beyond SOCCER MOM

"As a published author myself, I rarely see the kind of writing that captivates me from the first page, and *Beyond Soccer Mom* is one of those books. Dr. Leonaura Rhodes combines that talent with her knowledge of the tools that Moms need to be successful in their lives, fulfill their dreams and pull themselves out of a "mom" identity which we all seem to fall into at one point or another. *Beyond Soccer Mom* is not only an entertaining read, but a resourceful workbook to simply and efficiently guide any mother that needs a lift to live the life of her dreams!"

—**Judy Goss**, CEO of Over 40 Females

To: Theanne

Here's to a fabulous life!

Leonaura

beyond SOCCER MOM

Strategies for a Fabulous Balanced Life

DR LEONAURA
RHODES

NEW YORK

beyond SOCCER **MOM**
Strategies for a Fabulous Balanced Life

Published in New York, New York, by Morgan James Publishing. Morgan James and The Entrepreneurial Publisher are trademarks of Morgan James, LLC. www.MorganJamesPublishing.com

The Morgan James Speakers Group can bring authors to your live event. For more information or to book an event visit The Morgan James Speakers Group at www.TheMorganJamesSpeakersGroup.com.

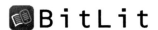

A FREE eBook edition is available
with the purchase of this print book

CLEARLY PRINT YOUR NAME IN THE BOX ABOVE

Instructions to claim your free eBook edition:
1. Download the BitLit app for Android or iOS
2. Write your name in UPPER CASE in the box
3. Use the BitLit app to submit a photo
4. Download your eBook to any device

ISBN 978-1-63047-137-8 paperback
ISBN 978-1-63047-138-5 eBook
ISBN 978-1-63047-139-2 hardcover
Library of Congress Control Number:
2014933864

Cover Design by:
Rachel Lopez
www.r2cdesign.com

Interior Design by:
Bonnie Bushman
bonnie@caboodlegraphics.com

In an effort to support local communities, raise awareness and funds, Morgan James Publishing donates a percentage of all book sales for the life of each book to Habitat for Humanity Peninsula and Greater Williamsburg.

Get involved today, visit
www.MorganJamesBuilds.com

DEDICATION

To Neil, who is my rock and my lovely boys Charlie
and Sam: you give me purpose and passion for life!

CONTENTS

ACKNOWLEDGMENTS

My first thanks go to Neil, Charlie and Sam thanks for your love, support, patience and gentle teasing while I was writing *Beyond Soccer Mom*.

Next, I'd like to thank every member of my amazing extended family, for your love, kindness, uniqueness and for being there for me over the years.

My huge thanks go to my family and friends who have helped edit *Beyond Soccer Mom*, whose advice was invaluable, particularly in helping point out when I was talking absolute nonsense.

Special thanks go to Mary Jane Reis, my talented editor, for her hard work, laser focus, good sense and outstanding advice.

INTRODUCTION

Beyond Soccer Mom is not just a book, it is an experience. The book is accompanied by a workbook and website, all designed to introduce you to a revolutionary new way of thinking. This book is for women who want a better life, for themselves and their families. The aim of *Beyond Soccer Mom* is to empower you to connect with your true self. It will dare you to dream and turn dreams into reality by taking positive action.

Who is "Soccer Mom"?

For the purposes of this book, the term "Soccer Mom" refers to any woman or mom who devotes her life to her family. Don't worry, you don't need to know anything about soccer to read this book, in fact, I will barely mention it again. If you are a woman who wants a better life, whether you stay at home, work part-time, full-time, or as an entrepreneur or business owner, this book is for you.

My research shows that many women, especially moms, are leading less than flourishing lives. I wonder if you ever feel:

- Unhappy
- Unhealthy
- Bored

- Overworked
- Stressed
- Frustrated
- Dissatisfied
- Under-employed
- Unemployable
- Like a door-mat
- Regretful
- Unfocused
- Disorganized
- Depressed
- Or that your family is dysfunctional?

If so, it's time to say hello to feeling:

- Happy
- Healthy
- Joyous
- Passionate
- Fulfilled
- Successful
- Focused
- Beautiful
- Organized
- Energetic
- Wealthy
- Fantastic
- And proud of your amazing family!

Why is *Beyond Soccer Mom* different?

I have a confession: I am a personal development junkie. I have read many of the thousands of personal development books out there that promise to change your life. I have also taken several personal development courses, seminars and webinars and have undergone tremendous personal growth. I am always left thinking, however that these books and courses don't take into account the busy and complicated lifestyle of moms.

What do I mean? Well, most moms can't spend 30 minutes meditating when they get up in the morning or drop everything and have a night off, every time they feel stressed. What works well for a single woman in her twenties or for the middle-aged man facing a career transition does not necessarily work well for a busy mom.

This is where *Beyond Soccer Mom* is different. Like you, I am a mom. While I can never truly understand YOUR life, I can understand some of your struggles. I have lived the emotional roller-coaster that is motherhood for the past 16 years. I am here to help YOU: the Mom, the CEO and pilot of your family. I am here to help you create the flourishing life that you deserve, a life filled with more happiness, passion, joy, health, success and abundance.

I am here to tell you that your dreams can become a reality. Your dreams may be small, like getting away for a weekend with a friend, or big, like setting up a business or writing a book. Do you think JK Rowling ever imagined her novel about an eleven-year-old boy would turn into the multimillion dollar industry that is now Harry Potter? Women are powerful, resourceful, resilient, creative, loving beings, capable of amazing things. What stands between you and your dreams is often just the simple process of creating a personalized road map for your life, and following it.

Beyond Soccer Mom will guide you to take three critical steps:

Rediscover your true identity, reignite your passion for life and dare to dream of an amazing future for you and your family.

Make a rock-solid plan to improve your life.

Get your body and mind into the best shape possible so that you will achieve positive, fast, long-lasting change in your life.

I will share personal and real life stories, from women and moms I have encountered and worked with over the last 16 years. The purpose of these stories is to show that *Beyond Soccer Mom* is not an academic exercise. It is for real women, like you, who want to changes in their lives for the better.

While *Beyond Soccer Mom* is not an academic exercise, my background, interest and research in the fields of coaching, medicine and neuroscience have had a major influence on the content.

The Conception of *Beyond Soccer Mom*

The concept for this book arose during coffee with two close friends, both stay-at-home moms. I consider myself to be a part-time coach and part-time stay-at-home mom, and there is always the danger when I am socializing that an idea for a book or course will pop into my mind. My friends mentioned that they were a little envious of me running my own business. I told them that it was hard work and that I sometimes wished I could be satisfied with being a stay-at-home mom, as they were. They went on to tell me that they were generally content and happy but sometimes felt bored and frustrated, and regretted leaving their old jobs behind. They said they often ended their day wondering where the time had gone and what they had achieved. There was always a new pile of dirty laundry, more dirty dishes to be washed and more piles of stuff to organize. Indeed, this was the feeling I had almost daily when I was a full-time stay-at-home mom. They said they loved their families and were glad to be around for all of those special moments: the Halloween parade at school, baby's first steps and that amazing soccer goal. However, there were times when they wondered about their futures; about what they would do if their husband lost his job, if their marriage suddenly ended or when their children had all left home.

I listened to them sharing their dreams and ideas: writing a book, setting up a tutoring service, running a business and returning to work. I asked them what was stopping them from turning their dreams and ideas into reality. Their answers were unsurprising: lack of time, "mommy-brain" (thinking that your brain doesn't work so well after having children), lack of focus, confidence and skills, and not knowing where to begin. I told them that I thought that what they actually lacked was motivation, focus and a really good plan. They laughed and agreed and soon we said our goodbyes.

The next day, one of the friends called me to say that she had told her husband that she was considering returning to work, and he agreed it was a wonderful idea. The problem was where to start. It seemed very overwhelming. I told her that our conversation had inspired me to create a coaching program. And so the Beyond Soccer Mom Program was born.

My two friends were my guinea pigs for the program. We met weekly for four weeks and both friends enjoyed the course, experiencing many insightful moments. Soon they began to take steps towards improving their lives. One set up a weekly date night with her husband and was researching setting up a tutoring service. The other had planned a surprise getaway for her family and signed up for a writing class to further her dream of becoming an author.

I have subsequently run the program many times. The feedback is always positive and the content always improving. For me it is a joy to work with such amazing women focused on building a wonderful future for themselves and their families.

In order to share my message and make it more affordable and accessible to many more women, the obvious next step was to create a book and here it is. Beyond Soccer Mom has been my baby, my passion and my focus for nine months. I hope you enjoy reading it as much as I have enjoyed writing it for you.

My promise to you

My intention is to help you build a wonderful life. If you read this book and take an active role by doing some of the exercises, you are likely to experience positive change and enhance your life. You may even have an increased sense of inner peace. If you do not, I want to hear from you.

Your promise to me

I have several promises to ask of you:

- Keep an open mind.
- Take responsibility.
- Dare to dream.

- Buy a journal.
- Download and use the workbook. In the book you will be given the instruction "complete the exercise", this means print and complete the appropriate exercise from the workbook.
- Try to read the whole book and do many of the exercises. You may think there are areas of your life which are fine just as they are, but there is always room for improvement or self reflection.
- Set aside some uninterrupted time to read the book and do the exercises: no e-mail, no cell phone, and no interruptions from your children. For you to benefit fully from the book, you must give it your full focus and attention.
- And finally TAKE ACTION!

Your journal

A number 2 pencil and a dream can take you anywhere
—Joyce Meyer

Acquire a journal solely for use with *Beyond Soccer Mom*. Raid your child's school supplies or go out and buy one. A simple school notebook will do or you may want to treat yourself to a fancy journal.

Throughout the book you are invited to write in your journal. There is a good reason for this, and it has to do with the way your brain works. When we think a thought, no matter how impressive it is, if we fail to give it adequate focus, our brain will fail to process it and act upon it.

There are two great ways to create focus on a thought: one is to discuss it with another person, and the other is to write it down. Writing down your thoughts is like having a conversation with your own subconscious mind. Writing activates several areas of your brain, making it more likely that you will remember and process the information.

Reviewing your journal scribbles at a later date will be enlightening. You will see how often thoughts, emotions and ideas change. You'll be amazed at how often you will think, "Did I really write that?"

The workbook

There are many exercises in this book, designed to aid you on your journey towards a flourishing life. To make life easier I have created The *Beyond Soccer Mom* Workbook. It is available as a complementary download at www.beyondsoccermom.com/workbook. I urge you to download this, right now, before we go on. Do it now! I'm waiting. Have you done it yet?

When you have downloaded it, save it in a memorable place on your computer, then print relevant exercises as you progress.

While you will get great value from just reading the book, your success will come from your active role in the process. If you complete the exercises and take positive action, you will begin a transformative journey that will empower you to create the life you and your family deserve and desire. If you follow the steps outlined, you are likely to experience significant change in your life.

As you do this work, remember this truth: when people fail to take personal responsibility and positive action towards well-defined goals, they tend to have regrets about what they have achieved. It is like they set out on a potentially wonderful journey, but with no destination in mind and no map.

Many moms regret wasting their best years, not meeting their own needs, not following their dreams, all because they believe they have to put their own life on hold when they are a mom. This old way of thinking is not the *Beyond Soccer Mom* way. Promise me that from this day forward you will live true to your authentic self, with passion, purpose, energy and drive and become one of the new generation of moms who knows their true value.

The website and the community

The website www.beyondsoccermom.com is designed to be an organic resource to accompany this book. Here you will find a wealth of additional information to support you. You will also find access to two communities for readers of *Beyond Soccer Mom*, so that you can share your experience with other moms.

A book of two parts

This book is designed to be like a cook book. The first part will teach you how to cook or how to decide what you want from life and then take positive, purposeful action. The second part will teach you easy-to-follow recipes for changing specific areas of your life. The recipes may be used flexibly and creatively. Unlike a cook book, however, you will benefit most from reading the whole book and doing those exercises that are relevant to you.

Before we start

A journey such as this requires a team. Your team may be friends, family or a coach. Close family members are one of your most precious resources. However, they may sometimes not understand your motivation for change. They may feel a little threatened by your desire to have a better life. They may wonder if they have let you down in some way, or fear that you might be less available to them in the future. It is important to reassure them that this is not the case. If you need help offering this reassurance, please ask them to read the following notes. The first is for the significant adult men in your life: your partner (as he will be known in the rest of the book), husband, boyfriend or fiancé. The second is for your children and is aimed at teenagers.

A note to men

Hello and thanks for taking the time to read this note. *Beyond Soccer Mom* is not about soccer, sorry if you are disappointed. It's a personal development book for women to help them become more happy, healthy and successful.

Firstly, I'd like to explain why I have written a book for moms. When I describe my book to men, they often say "but I could do with that too!" or "why are you writing it just for women?"

I have many reasons for writing a book for moms. Here are my top three.

- First off, I wanted to write a book for the group I most identified with and that is moms.
- The next reason is that the book morphed from a coaching course I run for moms, and I wanted to share the content with many more women.
- The third reason is that for the last 16 years of my life, since I became a mom, I have yearned for the type of advice and support offered in this book.

I would love you to read or skim this book and maybe try some of the exercises. Most are just as relevant to you as they are to the woman in your life. I have worked as a physician and coach with thousands of men and women. I enjoy coaching men just as much as women and it's my heart-felt belief that you too deserve more happiness, health and success in your life.

However, research shows that many moms are stressed, unhappy, unfulfilled and even bored. I first want to say, before you get defensive, that if this describes the woman in your life, it's probably not ALL your fault. In fact, it may not be your fault at all. Women go through periods, when they just feel they want more from life. If you believe that the woman in your life has little or no reason to feel this way, you must understand that, the way she feels has more to do with her personal perspective and the function of her brain and mind, than her physical circumstances. I'm sure you've heard of people who are rich and famous and appear to have it all, and yet are so incredibly unhappy. Some women will be reading this book not because they are unhappy or stressed but just because they enjoy experiencing personal growth, through reading.

Let's call the woman in your life your partner for simplicity. Your partner is not being selfish reading this book; she is reading it, because she knows that if she feels happier, healthier and more successful, she will be able to meet the needs of the people she loves, more easily. She will have more energy, be more productive, have better relationships and be inclined to have more fun, passion and adventure in her life.

Relationship guru John Gray's best-selling book *Men are from Mars, Women are from Venus*, is worth a read, if you struggle to understand women. He offers excellent advice to men. I have paraphrased it here:

- A woman's emotional state is like a wave, naturally flowing up and down. The flow of the wave can't be changed suddenly. Your partner is not going to stop being upset because you tell her she has no reason to be upset.
- When your partner complains and moans about her life, she is usually not blaming you or asking you to fix anything, she usually just wants you to listen and try to empathize. She may make assumptions that

you know how she is feeling and why. So if you sense that something is wrong, gently ask for clarification.

- Men and women speak a different language. It's not anyone's fault, they are just programmed that way. Women often like to use dramatic language to get their point across, and they rarely ask directly for help. They unconsciously prefer to drop hints. Your partner is more likely to say "I've had a terrible day. I am exhausted, and you never help out," than to say "please, could you unload the dishwasher? I am tired, and I need a five-minute break before I can do more."

- Woman love to feel cared for, listened to, understood, respected, validated, reassured and loved unconditionally, no matter how long you have been together. Most women appreciate multiple small gestures more than one large one. Of course your partner appreciates how hard you work, but she also needs frequent reminders that you care. Surprising her with the occasional romantic treat like flowers or dinner out, or offering to do chores when she's looking stressed or tired will score you extra points.

- When you feel stressed or need to withdraw, reassure her that you just need some time alone, so that she doesn't feel anxious that you have gone.

- If you are in a loving relationship, your partner will rarely hurt you on purpose and she may not be aware that you have been hurt by her actions. If she has hurt you, tell her so instead of withdrawing.

Paula and Bob's story

Paula came to see me early in January, very upset with her partner, Bob. It turned out that, for the fifteenth year running, he had bought her expensive jewelry for Christmas, and I mean expensive.

Wondering why Paula was so upset? Well, she had dropped many hints about the gift she really wanted: a day at a spa, a trip to the theatre and a new bottle of perfume. To her, the expensive jewelry was a poorly thought out, unnecessarily extravagant gift, which she didn't need or value. And so, again for the fifteenth year running, they had a huge argument on Christmas day. The poor guy!

At our session, we talked at length about her relationship with Bob. Paula acknowledged that she knew that Bob really loved her and worked very hard for the family. I explained that, to him, the gift was very significant; he had worked hard to earn that money and thought the jewelry would make her feel valued. I explained to her that she needed to be explicit about what she wanted and why she got upset about his gifts, as Bob was clearly not getting the hints she was offering. She went home that day and told him how she felt. He was so surprised and confused that she had never been honest about what she wanted, and why she always got cranky on Christmas day.

So as you can see, we women are complicated creatures, who are often not very good at expressing our wants, needs and feelings. So have a big favor to ask of you. While the woman in your life is reading this book, she may ask for some help. She may ask you to give your opinion on something, like "I'm thinking about taking a painting class, what do you think?" Or she may ask you to help out a little more with chores, so she is less stressed and frustrated. Most women do not enjoy or feel any sense of accomplishment from doing laundry. Please support her. There is nothing that I suggest in this book that should affect her relationship with you negatively, in fact, quite the opposite. The aim of this book is to help her increase wellbeing in all areas of her life, including her relationship with you.

Thanks in advance for supporting the woman in your life while she reads this book!

Leonaura

A note to children

Hi, thanks for reading this and supporting your mom. First to be clear, *Beyond Soccer Mom* is not about soccer! It's a book to help your mom become more happy, healthy and successful. You might think your mom is pretty much okay right now and that's great. Sometimes moms realize that while their life is okay, and they have a wonderful child like you, something is missing for them, something that would make their life a little bit better.

Your mom is not being selfish reading this book and doing the exercises. She just knows that if she feels happier, healthier and more successful, she will be a better mom, to you. She will have more energy, be able to help you out more, keep up with you better and have more fun with you.

I have a big favor to ask of you. While your mom is reading this book, she may ask for some help. She may ask for your advice on something, like "I'm thinking about taking a painting class, what do you think?" or she may ask you to help out a little with chores, so she is less stressed. Don't forget your mom just wants a better life for herself, for you and your family. So when she asks for your help please try and support her.

One other favor, I ask of you. Try every now and again to "put yourself in your mom's shoes." No, I am not asking you to wear her favorite heels! I am asking you to think about how your mom thinks and feels. If she asks you to do something you don't want to do, there's a good chance it's because she loves you. Here you may be saying "What is this silly woman talking about?" What I am talking about is the simple fact that most moms, most of the time, want their child to be happy, healthy and successful. So when she asks you, or even tells you, to do something, it's probably because she believes that in the long term it will benefit you.

Thanks in advance for supporting your mom while she reads this book!

Leonaura

Let's get started

When you are ready and fully engaged, I'd like you to join me on a journey towards creating a more fulfilling future for you and your family.

Chapter 1

A ROADMAP FOR CHANGE

My story

I have been a mother for 16 years. During this time I have worn many hats including: cleaner, cook, student, homework supervisor, babysitter, physician, teacher's assistant, counselor, life coach, support group leader, drain unblocker (yes, really), boy scout leader, party organizer, poop cleaner, parent teacher association chair, neurotherapist, soccer manager, and of course loving wife and mother.

I know it's a cliché, but motherhood has been an emotional roller coaster, a wild ride from the highs of joy, excitement, pride, unconditional love, gratitude, surprise and hope, through to the lows of depression, sadness, boredom, frustration, confusion, disappointment, grief and anxiety.

My life "before children" seems unreal, almost like it happened to someone else. You know how people say "I wouldn't change a thing"? Well I would! I would love to relive my days of parenting, knowing what I *know now. I would have loved to have had more help and guidance. I would have loved to have made fewer mistakes. I would have loved to have been a better wife and mother. I would have loved to experience more fun, energy, adventures and success.*

So, my purpose in writing this book is to help you travel the journey that is motherhood while keeping your sanity, intelligence, health and wellbeing intact.

The Problem

Being a mother is hard. There are so many conflicting demands on your time and energy. You may often feel like you are not doing a good job of anything. Many mothers find themselves wracked with feelings of fear, guilt, blame, worry, conflict, regret and inadequacy.

Whether you work full-time, part-time, from home or in the home, the balancing act can be very challenging.

Moms who work outside the home face the challenges of prioritizing the demands of work, home and family. They have to contend with child care, commuting tiredness, limited family time, and little or no "me time". In short, they cope with stress from many, many sources. There are some advantages, though, to working outside of the home. Research shows: "Work is good for [women's] health, both mentally and physically. It gives women a sense of purpose, self-efficacy, control and autonomy. They have a place where they are an expert on something, and they're paid a wage" (Frech, 2012).

Many outsiders may think that being a stay-at-home mom is idyllic. They believe that moms have an abundance of free time, to do whatever they like. From this assumption has arisen the patronizing phrase "ladies who lunch". The truth is however, that most stay-at-home moms lead busy, stressful lives and spend much of their time doing things they don't particularly enjoy. In my seminars, many moms report feeling bored, desperate, lonely, stressed, under-valued, under-productive, depressed and disorganized. Many feel that they have lost their identity and their passion for life. They often feel the pressure of money worries due to lack of income. Most stay-at-home moms can't afford or justify the expense of help in the home, and feel overwhelmed by the tedium and lack of satisfaction they gain from housework. When children are sick, disabled, having problems at school or fighting with siblings, the burden of being a stay-at-home parent can be a particularly heavy one.

So here's a question for you: "Are you one of those moms who puts meeting your own needs at the bottom your to-do-list?" If so, you know that's not okay, don't you?

In my "Magic Wand Survey," I asked moms what they wanted more of. They told me they wanted more happiness, travel, connection, laughter, love, patience, inspiration, financial security, free time, passion, joy, love, empowerment, energy, confidence, appreciation, inner peace, friendship, fun and quality time with their family. Does any of this ring true to you? Well I am here to tell you that you deserve all of those things in abundance. The great news is that you CAN have an amazing life, and I am here to be your guide.

The Solution: *Beyond Soccer Mom*

The aim of *Beyond Soccer Mom* is to help you design and act upon a plan that will:

1. Improve the health and wellbeing of your family. Now you may ask why I am putting this first. Surely the whole *Beyond Soccer Mom* concept is about YOU, not your family. Well, in my experience most mothers prioritize meeting their child's needs way above their own. So here's some motivation for you: experts agree that maternal depression and stress have an adverse effect on the development, health, wellbeing and success of children. Your child NEEDS you to be happy and healthy. When you fail to meet your own needs you are being selfish and harming your child. There, I've said it: harsh but true!

2. Increase your health, happiness, success and abundance. I have three questions for you. First question: "What will you do with your life if and when your last child leaves home?" Second question: "Are you ready for the many challenges life is going to throw at you?" And finally: "When you look back on your life will you say 'I led a truly great life?'" You deserve good health, happiness, success and abundance.

3. Empower you to be an outstanding role model for your child. For most children, mom is a principal role model for a healthy, happy, successful life.
4. To increase your contribution to your community, to the workforce or to creating excellent books, art, music, businesses and ideas, if you so desire.

To build resilience so that you can cope with whatever life throws at you.

Plan to succeed

Most people fail to achieve their goals because:

1. They are unclear about what they want to achieve and why,
2. They don't have a sound plan,
3. They are not physically or mentally prepared for change.

When we fail to achieve our goals, we become despondent, discouraged and negative. I believe it is important to set yourself up for success, not failure.

Consider your future life as a journey that you need to map out. When you create this map, you need to know a few things:

- Where you are starting (what your life is like, now)
- Your destination (what you want your life to be like)
- A good route (your plan for getting to your desired life)
- Your vehicle (your body and your health)

Drawing on my years of experience and research of coaching methods, neuroscience and medicine, I have developed the ASPIRE strategic map, to help you improve your life quickly, efficiently and effectively.

The ASPIRE Strategic Map

This map includes three main steps:

Step 1. To understand your "authentic self" or true identity. That is who you are and who you want to be.

Step 2. To plan change with integrity towards your authentic self.

Step 3. To learn to "regulate and empower" yourself by being in a peak performance state both physically and mentally, so that you increase your chances of success.

Oh, and if you really want to succeed in creating lasting change, you will need to do all three at once. Don't worry though: the three steps all support each other. If you do one, the other two will be easier.

ASPIRE: Strategic Map

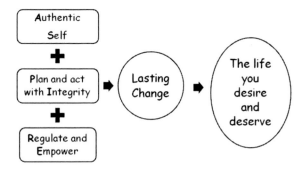

What is success?

Before we go further, we should define success clearly. Is an athlete only successful if they win a gold medal at the Olympics? No. They are successful every time they complete a run, set a new personal best and learn the latest technique. Is a business person only successful if they are CEO of the biggest company in the world? No. They are successful every time they have a business deal that goes well or when they exceed their profit forecast. Is a mother successful only if she produces the healthiest, cleverest child, ever? No. She is successful when she discovers a new hobby that makes her happy, when she helps her child recover from a nasty cold or when she gets to the bottom of the pile of ironing. My definition of success is "achieving progress towards your goals." Set goals that measure progress, that are achievable and realistic and that have a timescale. Then teach your family to do the same.

Julie's story

Julie had a successful career as a pediatric nurse but left work to stay home with her three children. After eight years, she came to see me feeling deeply unhappy about her career and family life. Several months prior, her husband, Max, had opened up and told her he was so worried about his job security; he thought she should return to work. At first Julie felt shocked and scared. However, as she thought about her situation, she realized she had really missed working as a nurse and often felt bored and dissatisfied staying at home.

Julie had kept up her nursing license, so after a short refresher course she was back in work, covering for a nurse, on maternity leave. Things went well for a few weeks: Julie had to get up at 6 a.m. to get her children ready for school. She would squeeze in some housework while making breakfast for the family. Her workday ran from 8.30 a.m. to 5.30 p.m. She employed a sitter to care for her children after school and to take on some of the housework. When she returned from work each night at around 6pm, her children greeted her and shared their news. Often there would be homework to help with and various after-school activities to attend. Then she had to make dinner, spend time with her husband, check email, pay bills and plow through the never ending cycle of housework. There were moments when she loved the work, when she was back in her "before children flow." Yet these times were rare and exhaustion quickly set in.

Then one day she got a call at 10am from the nurse at her eight year old's school. He had vomited in class and had to be collected, immediately. Max was traveling on business and she couldn't ask a friend to have a vomiting child. And so, with no one else to call, she made her apologies and left work. Her coworkers and head nurse were very understanding; it was a Pediatric Unit and they understood children get sick. That evening, however, spots appeared along with a fever: her son had chickenpox (children do not get immunized against chicken pox in the UK). For the next six miserable weeks, one child after the other got sick. Julie was only able to work two full days, in those weeks, when Max could work from home. Her employers were very understanding, even though it put huge pressure on the other staff. She felt terrible about letting her colleagues down, and she could sense resentment building. But soon she returned to work and resumed the cycle.

Then the summer break arrived with all of its additional challenges: juggling childcare, trying to fit in a family vacation and grappling with huge additional childcare costs. Worst of all: Julie felt that she was missing out, on precious time with her children.

Julie's temporary contract was coming to an end when she came to see me. She had been offered a full-time job in the clinic. She was glad to have returned to work: she enjoyed the buzz of being part of a team and felt good about doing the job she was trained for. But Julie knew she was becoming depressed and overwhelmed. She constantly worried about her children getting sick and their school grades dropping, and she felt that she was missing out on seeing them grow up. Julie had put on weight because she had no time to exercise and she had not been out with friends for several months. The final straw came when she realized that, after expenses, she was earning less money than her sitter.

So began the process of helping Julie to decide what to do next. We began by exploring her "authentic self": her personal story, her perspective, what she valued and what she wanted from life. Then, with a clear picture of the life she desired, we constructed a plan. The fundamental aim was to increase Julie's health, happiness, success, wealth and sense of balance in her life. We also worked on improving her physical and emotional wellbeing, so that she could be in a peak state when it was time to take action. We will follow Julie throughout this book.

So now that you understand the *Beyond Soccer Mom* model, let's get started with your strategic map.

Chapter 1 Summary

If you are not happy, healthy and successful, you have a problem. The solution lies in *Beyond Soccer Mom*.

The aim of *Beyond Soccer Mom* is to:

1. Improve the health and wellbeing of your family.
2. Increase your health, happiness, wealth and success.
3. Empower you to be an outstanding role model for your child.
4. Get you back into contributing beyond yourself and your family.
5. Build your resilience so that you can cope with whatever life throws at you.

The ASPIRE strategic map will help you create lasting change and the life you desire. It has three steps:

1. Get to know your "Authentic Self"
2. Plan change with Integrity towards your authentic self
3. Regulate and Empower yourself by getting in a peak state of mental and physical health.

Remember: Success is achieving progress towards your goals.

Chapter 2

↷ AUTHENTIC YOU ↶

Two of the most profound questions you can ask of yourself are: "who am I?" and "what makes me who I am?"

Not surprisingly, these are very difficult questions for most of us to answer. Who we are, is determined our unique genetics, our environment and how we have processed the events and experiences in our lives. You think differently, see differently, hear differently, feel differently, interpret differently and even taste and smell differently from every other person on the planet. Likewise, you have your own profile of needs, passions, values, attitudes and beliefs which influence how you live your life.

Authentic self

The term "authentic self" is used in psychology, spirituality and eastern religions. It refers to who you are at your core, free from assumptions. It is uniquely yours. Yet over time, many of us lose touch with our authentic selves. I have seen this sense of loss of self, in many of the moms I have coached.

Yet moms, perhaps more than anyone else, need to have a strong sense of self. Why? Because the better you can identify with, understand and listen to the voice of your authentic self, the more likely you are to be happy, content and energetic. In turn this positivity will spill over to your children, your family and your community.

The process of understanding your authentic self is not a simple one, however. Your authentic self is constantly changing and evolving. Like a tree across the seasons, the true self is endlessly influenced by the weather of life, that is to say the constant changes around you and within you. There is no right or wrong way to connect with your authentic self. Methods include spiritual study, reading personal development books, attending a yogic retreat and personal coaching.

This book, and in particular this chapter, aims to be one starting point, for your journey towards better understanding your authentic self. I promise you will not be asked to engage in unnecessary navel gazing or self indulgence. You will be guided through a process of honest self-reflection, to discover the hidden source of your authentic self, which will guide you towards a meaningful, fulfilling life.

What your authentic self is not

While it is important to know what authentic self is, it's just as important to know what it is not. Authentic self should not defined by any one aspect of who you are, like your role, education, job, location or wealth. Nor should it be defined by what society or other people think of you, including your spouse and children. Your authentic self should not be defined by comparisons to other people, whether the comparison involves your older sister or your predecessor at work. Your authentic self precedes and supersedes all of these external perceptions and preoccupations.

Facets of authentic self

Like leaves on a tree, there are many thousands of facets to your authentic self. Let's consider seven key facets:

- Personal Perspective
- Values
- Strengths and weaknesses
- Passions

- Needs
- Purpose
- Thought patterns

Authentic Self

Personal Perspective

Everything we hear is an opinion, not a fact.
Everything we see is a perspective, not the truth
—Marcus Aurelius

We have all heard stories of positive, successful people who endured terrible adversity early in their lives. For example, people living in concentration camps, people born with physical disability or people who have experienced unimaginable loss. For each one of those positive and successful people, there are probably many more that experienced similar adversity and went on to become despondent, hopeless and defeated. The major difference between these two types of people is their perspective.

We all have our own special way of seeing the world. Have you ever wondered whether other people see colors the same way you do? I have a friend who perceives different days as having different colors. She says it's like wearing glasses with different colored lenses each day. Our perspective is the lens through which we see the world. If you wake up one day with a headache, bump your head and then stub your toe, you might view the rest of the day through a negative lens. Whereas, if you wake up, on vacation in a beautiful place, with your loved ones around you, you might see the rest of your day through a positive lens.

Your perspective is quite unique, determined by not only by what you are sensing or experiencing in the moment, your current state of mind and the context of the experience but also what you have experienced and processed previously. Your journey up until now has no doubt had its highs and lows. Some of these lows have been totally out of your control, others you may in part be responsible for. It is important to acknowledge your journey up to now, both to learn lessons from your past and to make a conscious decision to not let your past hinder you any longer.

The problem with your perspective is that it is your reality, but it may not always be accurate and may in fact, be harming you. The good news is that with self reflection and better understanding of your authentic self and your place in the world, you can shift your perspective, to become more positive and helpful.

My perspective

In my early 30s, I made the difficult decision to leave my job and become a stay-at-home mom, to care for my sons, who had were both very ill. During this stressful period in my family life, I became quite depressed. Worse yet, I became envious and resentful of a friend, who seemed to be having such an easy time. Like me, she had two children, but both were fit and well with barely a snuffle between them. Her husband also worked with mine, until he was offered a new job with a huge salary. We were not badly off, but for me this was just adding another injustice to the situation. I began to obsess about her good fortune and my apparent bad luck. My obsessing made me very unhappy.

Then one day I discovered the book The Art of Happiness by HH Dalai Lama and Howard C. Cutler. The authors retell a tale from Buddhist tradition of a woman who suffered the death of her only child. The woman went to bargain with Buddha for the return of her child. Buddha told her that there was a medicine that would bring her child back to life. In order to receive it, she must bring to him, mustard seeds collected from three families unaffected by death. Her quest was unsuccessful and she made a decision to move on with her life. The message I took from this story was this: Loss and misfortune are universal, not personal. But suffering is optional.

My perspective shifted in a heartbeat. I felt like a shadow had lifted from my life. As I read on, my perspective on other issues changed too. The authors explained that negative thoughts such as jealousy, hatred, blame and regret serve only to harm the person who thinks them. Every person will experience negative events. However, these negative events don't define us; only our responses do. I chose in that moment to see the positives in my life, to find new purpose and to take responsibility for my future.

Your true power lies in deciding where you want your future to take you, creating a plan and then taking positive action.

The past

The events of your past and your perspective on them deeply influence who you are. The following exercise will help you consider your past, the events that have occurred and how they affected you.

Exercise 2.1 Time Line

Step 1. Take a fresh piece of paper A4 or bigger and draw a line in the middle of the page or print the exercise. There is an example at the end of the instructions. Write in pencil and have an eraser handy.

Step 2. At the very left of the line draw a cross and write "Birth" or something similar. It's your timeline, be creative. Add the date.

Step 3. At the very right of the line draw a cross and write "now" or something similar. Add the date.

Step 4. Think about the major events in your life which are significant to you, today. They may be small events, such as passing your first dance exam, or big, like the loss of relative. Write positive events above the line, negative below. Draw a line between the event and the time line, the length being proportionate to the significance.

ONLY WHEN YOU HAVE FINISHED READ STEP 5

Step 5. Look at the events you have marked. Ask yourself:
* Would everyone interpret this event in the same way?

Step 6. For any negative events ask:
* Have I now come to terms with this event?
* Is there a new, more positive way that I could view this event?

Exercise: Time Line

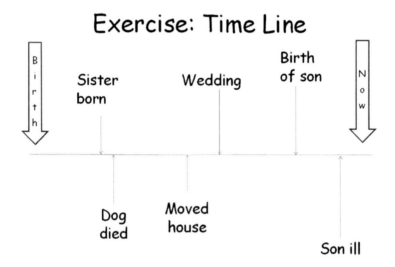

The now

Consider your life now. Once again, your perspective influences how you view your life, in the present. There are many people in the world that are living in absolute poverty, without assured access to the basics (food, water, shelter, clean air) and who are, nonetheless, happy and content. The reverse is also true: There are extremely wealthy, "successful" people who are miserable and dissatisfied with their lives.

The next exercise will help you evaluate your perspective on your life now. There are as many versions of this exercise as there are coaches and it goes by many names. My model has evolved with me, over several years, as my knowledge and experience has grown.

Exercise 2.2 Wheel of Life

Wheel of Life

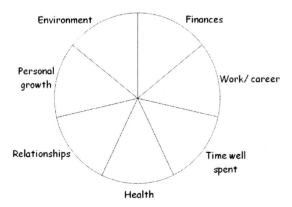

Complete the exercise or copy out the wheel into your journal.

Step 1. Think about your level of satisfaction or contentment today or in the last week in regard to these seven aspects of your life or "life assets".

- Finances: how certain you feel about your financial future? Consider your overall financial situation, rather than the amount of money you have.

- Work/career: how content you are with what you currently do, whether you are a stay-at-home mom or you work inside or outside of the home?

- Time well spent: do you feel you have spent your time well at the end of each day or week?

- Health: how content are you with your physical and mental health and with the health related lifestyle choices you make?

- Relationships: How are the major relationships in your life faring? Consider the quality of the significant relationships in your life.

- Personal growth: do you feel that you are growing, progressing or developing as a person?

- Environment: consider your physical environment (your country through to your home) and your life situation (perhaps you are experiencing a major life event).

Step 2. Rate the level of satisfaction for each life asset. 10 = extremely satisfied, 1 = totally dissatisfied. Then of course any other score in between 1 and 10.

Step 3. Put a dot in the center of the segment of the wheel to represent your level of satisfaction, 1 = as close to the middle as you can get, 10 = on the outside of the wheel, 5 = in the middle.

Step 4. Join each dot to the neighboring two dots to form a shape.

ONLY WHEN YOU HAVE FINISHED GO ON TO STEP 5

Step 5. Analyzing your wheel

- A small symmetrical wheel = you either have a lot of significant problems in your life or you have low self-confidence or depression. If you think you may have depression, I would recommend visiting your doctor. If you do not have depression, then you may need to work on improving your mindset (see Chapter Four)
- A large symmetrical wheel = you are either very fortunate or you are a positive thinker.
- An asymmetrical wheel = you have some areas of your life that are good right now and others that are not so good. The shape of your wheel provides a big clue as to what areas of your life you may need to focus on.

I have completed this exercise several times and it is always enlightening. When I compare my timelines, they are often very different. Some events drop off the list or their significance changes. In reality, the events have not changed, just my perspective.

I know this sounds obvious but you can't change the past. You can, however, always change your perspective on the past. In Chapter 4, you will get some help changing any negative thinking that might be affecting your life perspective.

Julie's Wheel

Julie first came to see me about losing weight, a problem with "Health". At first, this seemed a sensible place to start. She had gradually gained weight over the last few years and was becoming increasingly worried about her health, as there was a strong family history of diabetes. However, completion of her Wheel of Life revealed that she was most dissatisfied with "Career," "Time well spent" and "Relationships." It was dissatisfaction with these life assets that was causing the problems with her health; thus before we could address Julie's weight, we needed to prioritize these areas. If I had taken the problem at face value, we would have missed the causes of the "Health" problem and veered off in an unhelpful direction.

Wheel of Life: Julie

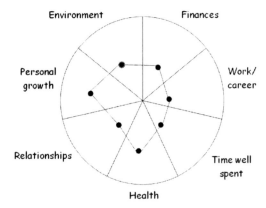

Values

Our values are the personal rules we live by and which give our life meaning. We each have our own unique value system, yet it is likely that you share some of your core values with your family and close friends. Spending time with people who have a very different value system can make you feel uncomfortable, even alone.

The problem with your value system is that you may not be consciously aware of it and living in conflict with your value system can make you feel dissatisfied, unhappy and unsuccessful.

Your value system has undoubtedly undergone some change throughout your life. The things you valued when you were a love-struck teenager are likely very different from what you value now, as a busy mom.

Bringing your value system into conscious awareness is a key step to knowing your authentic self. Your values affect what you say, think and do. Awareness of them may motivate and empower you, and prevent procrastination and self-sabotage. If you act in accordance with your value system, you will feel more content and confident.

"Core values" are those values critical to you and your wellbeing. The exercise that follows will help you get clarity about what you value and help you identify your core values.

Exercise 2.3 Value System
Short version
In your journal answer these questions:
- What's important in life, to me?
- What do I value most?
- Why?
- What could I not live without?

Longer version
Complete the exercise.

Go through the list and mark in column one anything you value.

When you have completed the whole list put a star next to your top ten.

Next pick your top three.

If you find this hard, pick two values at a time and ask yourself: "which of these would hurt me most to live without?"

On a separate piece of paper, write in large letters "I VALUE…" followed by your top three values. Put this piece of paper where you will see it every day, like on your bathroom mirror.

Ask yourself:

"Have I been living true to my values?" If the answer is "NO" consider the consequences?

For 20 days review your values.

Whenever you are making a decision of any importance, take a look at your value system. Ask yourself: "Will this decision support my values or go against them?"

Strengths and weaknesses

Now to consider what you are good at and what you are not so good at. Exploring strengths and weaknesses is not an exercise in self-adulation or boastfulness. Nor is it an exercise in self-loathing or negativity. Examining strengths and weaknesses is about honesty and self-acceptance. We all have our good points and bad points; they don't make us better or worse than anyone else, just different. The following exercise will help you identify your strengths and weaknesses.

Exercise 2.4 Strengths and Weaknesses

Complete the exercise or write in your journal. For each of the following statements rate whether it is: 1 = a big weakness, 2 = a small weakness, 3 = neither a strength nor a weakness, 4 = a small strength or 5 = a big strength.

- I get on well with other people
- I am a good communicator
- I am a good listener
- I set high standards for myself
- I achieve my objectives
- I am compassionate
- I am productive
- I am diligent at my work
- I take time to relax
- I manage my finances well
- I take care of my health
- I have no bad habits
- I am self reliant
- I eat sensibly
- I exercise regularly

- I am optimistic
- I am emotionally stable
- I have high self-esteem
- I am confident
- I am competent at what I do
- I am mainly happy
- I am tidy and organized
- I am prompt and reliable
- I don't need the approval of others
- I am well organized at home
- I am well organized at work
- I am a good parent
- I am a good intimate partner
- I am a good friend
- I am good with technology
- I am creative
- I have good attention to detail
- I am good at managing the home
- I am good at achieving balance in my life
- I am a good leader
- I am good at following instructions
- I am good at finishing tasks
- Other

Next answer the following questions:

- My top strengths are…
- How did they become strengths?
- How can I use my strengths more?
- Ways I use my strengths every day…
- Ways I can use my strengths more in the future…
- My biggest weaknesses are…
- How have they held me back or harmed me?

- Do I want to overcome them and why? (Some weaknesses aren't relevant to you, so you needn't worry about them).
- What will I need to do to turn this weakness into a strength, or to lessen the harm it causes?

You will be more efficient, productive and successful if you spend time doing tasks that play to your strengths.

In the book Strengths Finder 2.0, author Tom Rath suggests we should focus solely on strengths because, "people have several times more potential for growth when they invest energy in developing their strengths instead of correcting their deficiencies." While I understand this sentiment, I think you may benefit from identifying and addressing your weaknesses. If you ignore them they may come back to haunt you or sap your energy. For example I have tried many times to focus on my strengths, but my weak organizational skills always cause problems, unless I continue to focus time and energy on overcoming them.

If you have some weaknesses that you want to address urgently, complete exercise 3.1 "Personal Development Plan" (Chapter 3) in order to eliminate or reduce the impact of this weakness.

Passion

Passion is a strong emotion. It can be positive like love or negative like hate. Passion can increase your inspiration, drive and energy. Passion focuses and arouses your brain and body, putting it in an alert state. According to business coach Marie Forleo, there are two ways to become passionate: one is to figure out what you are already passionate about; the other is to become passionate about what you already do.

Thinking passionately

You may have been reminded of some of your passions doing the "Values System" and "Strengths and Weaknesses" exercises. Some passions are things you do often or things that you yearn to do. For example you might be passionate about cats, or about sewing and buy every new book on the subject.

The things you hate can be just as powerful as the things you love. If you can turn a passionate hatred for something into a passionate love for its' opposite, then you can use passionate energy to good effect. For example: if you hate being ill, then you become passionate about being fit and healthy. If you hate being bored, get actively engaged in an activity which excites you.

Exercise 2.5 Finding your passion
Complete the following statements:

- Things I love…
- Things I hate…
- Things I am obsessed with…
- Things I am passionate about…
- Things I would like to be passionate about…
- Things I am passionate about having…
- Things I am passionate about avoiding…
- Uses for my passions…

Becoming passionate
Your level of passion is linked to the meaning you give something and your level of engagement. If you want to get more done and be more efficient, try becoming more passionate. First give whatever you are doing some positive meaning and then get fully engaged and focused.

Example: Doing laundry
Positive meaning: I am doing a valuable task for my family because I love them and it feels really great to know I am up to date with the laundry.

Engagement: Focus on doing the laundry, be determined to do a good job of it. Say to yourself "I'm really good at doing the laundry."

Exercise 2.6 Becoming Passionate
Pick an activity that you do every day and don't enjoy.

Next time you do the activity; write down all of the positive meanings for this task.

Do the activity with full focus and attention. Do it to the best of your ability. Do the best job you have ever done. Notice the excellent job you are doing. Say out loud "I am such an expert at…"

If you start to lose focus, say the positive meaning out loud and refocus.

What do you notice?

My passion

For the nine months I spent writing this book, it was my passion! I even called it "my baby" at times. The positive meaning of this book for me, is that it brings together so many of my passions: I love coaching, I love helping people, I love writing, I love creating and I'm obsessed with health and neuroscience (just ask my kids). When I sat down to write, I did not read email or social media, and I did not think about housework. I set aside blocks of at least one hour, in which to write, when my children were at school or busy for long periods. Within five minutes I would be in "flow," and the words would come streaming out. The time would pass frustratingly quickly. I never procrastinated or complained about writing. When I was socializing, I couldn't help but mention "I'm writing a book," and I would talk about it with passion and energy. Most people I told would say "I need that now," even the men. You see passion is contagious!

Needs

We all have things in our life that we "need" in order to survive and flourish.

The most well-known model of "need" is Maslow's Hierarchy of Needs. Abraham Maslow, a developmental psychologist, came up with his "Theory of Human Motivation" in 1943. It is still used in many fields of practice from medicine to psychology, from business management to human resources. Maslow described five levels of need from the most basic physiological needs, safety, love and belonging, esteem, and finally self-actualization.

Another useful model comes from Human Needs Psychology, created by Tony Robbins and Chloe Maddanes. This model involves six human needs: certainty, variety, significance, love and connection, growth and contribution.

My own model draws on my experience as a coach and physician and has been refined over years of coaching.

Our Needs

The Need for Health

While you might not be sitting reading this book thinking "I need to be more healthy", you may be wishing you had more energy, more get-up-and-go, more focus or "to feel good". These are subtle markers of health.

Having worked with thousands of people and families affected by poor health, I firmly believe that the need for good physical and emotional health is of paramount importance. Poor health has a negative effect on your ability to meet all of your other needs. Conversely, good health makes it easier to focus on meeting your other needs and the needs of your loved ones.

Your body requires air, water, nutrition, sleep, homeostasis (regulation of the body's environment and function) and excretion. Above or below certain threshold levels of these requirements, your body will cease to function, and you will die. Even within a healthy range, these requirements affect the quality of your health. If you feel uncertain that your basic health needs will be met, you will feel driven to meet them.

One of the problems with health needs is that the signs of ill health are often easy to miss, at least in the early stages. For example, there are thousands of causes for fatigue ranging from lack of quality sleep through to cancer and diabetes. Another problem is that sometimes to meet the need to "feel good": to feel happy, motivated, energetic or focused, people take drugs or take part in activities which are a quick fix but in the long term are harmful to health.

The Need for Certainty

Certainty begins with the need to feel physically safe and protected. It also includes the need for certainty regarding other aspects of wellbeing, such as economic security, job security and social relationships (all discussed further in later chapters). Some people need a high level of certainty. Other people need low levels of certainty and crave variety, excitement and fun.

The Need for Connection and Love

The need for connection, belonging and love is very strong in most human beings and is closely linked to emotional health. This need can be met by interactions with family, friends or an intimate partner. It can also be met in social groups, such as a mom's group, a social media community or at work.

The love and connection a mom feels to her child is quite unique. For most moms, at least in the early years, this love is unconditional and begins before her baby is even born. The way a child expresses their connection and love to mom can vary considerably and change with age. A child's need for love and connection evolves during the teenage years and into adulthood, as they become more independent and begin creating relationships outside of the family.

As parents, we need to tune into the specific way our loved ones like to give and receive love and connection. An extreme variation can be seen in some children with special needs and autism, who need love and connection just like other children, but due to sensory, language, social and behavioral difficulties may prefer unusual ways of being shown love and connection. They may show less or atypical reciprocation of their parent's love and connection, compared to other children. These differences can be hard for some parents to come to terms with and positive parenting can be challenging.

The Need for Esteem

Humans need to feel good about themselves: to feel self-confidence and self-respect. This self-esteem can be enhanced by celebrating our strengths and successes, gaining knowledge, competence and mastery, being independent and self sufficient and having a sense of our own uniqueness. We also need to feel significant to others: that they need us, value us and respect us.

Sometimes we may meet the need for esteem in positive ways, like getting a qualification, celebrating a significant birthday, volunteering or sharing a funny story with friends. If, however, we have grown up with low level self-esteem, we may subconsciously develop the habit, of meeting this need in negative ways. Negative ways to meet our need for esteem include aggressive, violent or manipulative behavior but may also include telling people how depressed you are, sharing gossip or being nasty to other people.

The Need for Growth

The need for growth is the need to achieve your potential. It is the desire to grow, to experience, to accomplish, to achieve, and to create. This may include the need for spiritual growth, or the need to feel connected with something beyond yourself and your immediate circle of relationships. This spiritual need can be met through connection with god, humanity, nature or the universe. Malsow noted that you could survive without growth, but you would be unlikely to flourish or be truly content.

The Need for Contribution

Contribution to others can be a great source of happiness and esteem. When your basic needs are met, you may feel drawn to contributing. You may satisfy this need by caring for your family, or you may go beyond those bounds, to contribute to your church, your community, to charity, to politics and so on.

Problems with your needs

Consciously we may be unaware of how our needs drive us, yet they operate subconsciously as a script for our lives, causing several potential problems:

- You are often not conscious of how your needs drive your actions, behaviors and thoughts. For example, when you exercise, you don't specifically think "I need to meet my health needs."
- Sometimes people strive to meet their needs in a negative way. For example, some people meet their need for esteem by being violent, aggressive or loud. This extreme behavior makes them feel significant and important because people notice them. Children often behave negatively in order to meet their needs because they don't know how to meet the need positively. For example, if a child feels unloved and ignored, they may have a tantrum, do something naughty or pretend to be ill. If it works once, then why not try it again? Before long the problem behavior becomes a habit (more on habits later). Finding positive ways to meet our needs is one of the keys to success.
- People can become overly focused and rigid about meeting a need, to the extent that it causes harm. For example Suzie escaped from an emotionally and physically abusive marriage. In the years that followed, she was depressed and panicked anytime anyone got close

to her. Instead of focusing on her emotional wounds, she threw herself into a stressful job for a charity, which met her needs for esteem, growth and contribution. She became a self-confessed helicopter mom, over-mothering and spending excessively on her children. In these ways, she protected her need for physical and mental health, and her need for certainty. Yet she knew something was missing. She yearned for love and connection at a higher, more intimate level, but her drive to meet her need for safety and certainty stunted her emotional growth.

• Sometimes your needs may be met at a higher level than you desire. For example, caring for a sick family member may cause you to become overly focused on meeting health and certainty needs, to the extent that you have little fun, variety or growth in your life. Some children feel their need to growth is being met at a higher level, than they would ever desire by having to attend school, complete homework and attend after-school activities, causing them to push back and rebel.

What moms need

Remember those carefree days, when you had little responsibility and you could put your own needs first? When you could go out with friends and come back late, eat dessert for dinner or watch whatever you like on TV?

Then maybe your partner came along and, in order to allow the relationship to grow, you had to put your partner's needs above your own. Did you ever go on a date to a terrible restaurant or watch a dreadful movie, just to please your partner?

Then, even more significantly, your child or children came along. Suddenly, your own needs became less significant. Baby's needs had to be put first. Your baby needed to be fed, changed, entertained and generally cared for, often at times that were quite frankly inconvenient to your needs. Did you ever have to put off eating, despite feeling dizzy with hunger, because it was your baby was howling to be fed? Or wake up in the middle of the night, to soothe your child, even though you had slept only a few hours?

Right from the start, many moms get in the habit of neglecting their own needs, and they persist in this habit long past the point of necessity. Thus, the habit of self-neglect becomes ingrained and, left unchecked, causes great harm. You know when you are listening to the safety announcement on a plane, and they say put on your own oxygen mask before helping anyone else? Well being a truly good mom is like that. You must value your own needs so that you can adequately meet the needs of your family.

I have worked with many moms who have had demanding, sick or special needs children, as well as moms with big families. Many struggle to meet their family's needs, leaving little time to meet their own. When my son was sick in hospital, I collapsed with exhaustion and undiagnosed pneumonia because I was hadn't slept or eaten properly for over a week. If you are a mom who gives until it really hurts, make a promise to meet your own needs. Believe me, it's not a selfish act. An exhausted, depressed, ill mom is like a chocolate teapot, no use to anyone! Only when you value meeting your own needs, will you truly be able meet the needs of the people you love.

If you ever feel guilty because you don't contribute beyond your family, think again. The contribution you make to your family is an investment in their future and in society. If you do a good job of raising your children, they will contribute for many years to come. When they are grown and independent of you, then will come your time to contribute beyond your family, if you so desire.

The next exercise will help you identify your needs profile.

Exercise 2.7 My Needs Profile

Complete the exercise or copy the wheel into your journal. This wheel is similar to the Wheel of Life. Consider the level at which each of your six needs are being met.

Give each need a score. 1 = not being met at all 10 = being met completely.

Put a dot in the segment for each need. 1 = at center, 10 = on outside.

Ask yourself: "At what level would I like this need to be met?"

Put a cross in the segment for your desired level. Draw a line between the current and desired levels.

What is the gap?

My Needs

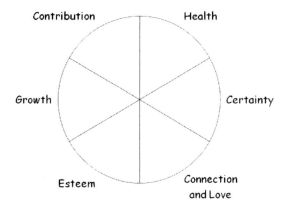

Complete the MY NEEDS Table with information from your wheel and answer the following additional questions:

Rank the order of importance of YOUR needs.

How do you currently meet each need? Consider whether you meet the need in a positive or a negative way.

Brainstorm ideas on how you could meet this need closer to your desired level.

If you have a big gap in one of the areas, I would recommend you complete Exercise 3.1 "Personal Development Plan" (Chapter 3).

Conflicting Needs

This is all very well but meeting your own needs and meeting the needs of your family can sometimes be tricky. Members of a family rarely share the same "needs profile" and this can cause complications. Imagine this family, planning a vacation:

- Mom desires health, certainty and growth. On vacation, she likes taking yoga classes, reading and eating healthy, local food.
- Dad desires a low level of certainty and a high need for growth. On vacation, he likes mountain biking, visiting historical sites and eating in expensive restaurants.

- Son has a low need for certainty and high need for esteem. On vacation, he likes to try the latest adrenaline sport, ride the scariest roller coaster and eat junk food.
- Daughter desires connection, love and certainty. On vacation, she loves nothing more than sitting by a pool sunbathing and chatting. Eating out is a challenge because she is very fussy.

Finding activities or vacations that meet the needs of all four family members would be quite a challenge. Some or all members of the family need to compromise in order to make the vacation successful.

If your family is in conflict over a major decision, such as a big move, consider asking each family to complete a "Needs Profile". This will help you understand the needs of each family member and consider how they can be met in your current situation, but don't forget you are the parent and have the final say.

Julie's values, strengths, weaknesses, passions and needs

Julie's top five values turned out to be love, health, certainty, family and growth. Her return to work had increased her feeling of growth but decreased her health and experience of love and certainty. Most significantly, her return to work had made her worry about the health of her family. She had been putting financial security, achievement, feeling valued, respect and making a difference above her top values. She now understood why returning to work had made her so unhappy: her values and behavior were out of alignment. Julie now realized she must consider "Values System" when planning change in the future.

Julie's strengths were related to interpersonal skills and therefore, her career choice of nursing was a good one. Her weaknesses lay in organizational skills and, as a result, her work-life balance was affected. Our coaching sessions included work to improve organizational skills, opening up time for higher value activities, like having fun with her children.

Julie confirmed that she had a passion for improving the health and wellbeing of children. She read avidly about child development and health and took courses on these subjects for pleasure. What's more, when she was working with children, the time seemed to fly by.

In contrast to her passion for children, Julie felt challenged by household chores. In short, she did not enjoy them and struggled to motivate herself. For this reason, she did the "Becoming Passionate" exercise for three weeks and reached a stage where she no longer resented housework and sometimes even enjoyed it.

Julie's "Needs Profile" was very enlightening. She admitted that, for several years, she had ignored her own needs, putting her family's needs above her own. The result? She had become over-focused on certainty (being overly anxious and protective of her children) and under-focused on having fun and enjoying life. Even worse, she was in poor health, had developed low self-esteem, mainly due to her difficulties with returning to work. Yet, when she didn't work, she did not feel that she was growing intellectually or spiritually. Returning to work increased her feeling of growth, but it was too much, too fast. Her need for connection and love was being met at a high level by her children, but she was concerned that her relationship with her husband had lost its sparkle. Her brief return to nursing had satisfied her need for contribution, but the cost was high.

These exercises helped Julie realize that returning to nursing was a good decision on many levels, but she needed to find ways to create a healthy balance between family and work commitments. More on Julie's journey later.

Your identity

Identity is "being who you are." In social science terms, it is your personal, social and cultural identity. However, identity is rather like an onion: at the core is your authentic self surrounded by the layers of other aspects of your life, like your role, age, education, job, location, wealth and what other people think of you. High self-esteem, resilience and emotional wellbeing will arise when identity is built on a strong sense of authentic self.

Exercise 2.8 Who am I?

Ask yourself:

"How would I introduce myself to a stranger?" Is it positive or negative?

"How would my child, partner, ex or closest friend introduce me, to a stranger?" Ask them if you dare.

"How would my community or culture describe me?"

Sit comfortably and put your hand on your heart and take some deep breaths. Connect with your authentic self. Consider your perspective on your life, so far, your values, your strengths, your passions, your needs. Now ask your authentic self "Who am I?" and "who do I want to become?"

My identity

One of the most upsetting experiences I had as a stay-at-home mom happened at a wedding. I had just begun to recover from a deep depression that had arisen due to my sons' illnesses and my decision to leave medicine. For the first time in a long while, I was ready to party. My confidence was pretty shaky, however. I had piled on several pounds due to emotional eating and felt fat and frumpy. Still a party is a party, and I made up my mind to have fun!

By mid-evening, I was having fun, catching up with old friends and dancing. Then one of the other guests introduced himself, and we began the usual polite wedding chatter. We discussed the lovely weather and our connection to the bride and groom. Then he asked "So what do you do?" I replied "I'm a stay-at-home mom…" I knew his girlfriend was a doctor, so I was just about to mention that I was taking a career break from medicine, when he turned his back and walked away. I felt like I had been punched in the stomach.

Three years later, on my first day of counselor training, I introduced myself to the other students, "Hi I'm Leonaura and I'm a stay-at-home mom, my kids were both very ill when they were young…. I have had depression but am recovering. I want to help other people recover from depression"

I listened to the other fascinating stories told by the other students. After the class, the tutor asked to see me. She said "I am very worried about you.

I think you may have lost sense of identity." I sat in the car before I drove home and cried. My tutor was right: I had totally lost sight of who I was. I had become a mother of two sick children and that was how I now defined myself. It was the last time I ever did that.

You can choose how to create your identity. When you do, make sure it is a positive one.

The future

Your future is a blank canvas. Sure, there will be many things in your future that you won't be able to control. But you can always control your perspective and reaction to the events in your life. You can choose to make your future decisions, thoughts and actions true to your authentic self and to choose a more flourishing life.

Ask yourself: "Do I deserve to be happy, healthy and successful?" If the answer is anything other than a resounding YES, then let me tell you are wrong. Of course you deserve this, everybody does, especially an amazing person like you!

Exercise 2.9 I deserve...
Take a fresh page in your journal and write in big beautiful letters:
   "I deserve to be happy, healthy and successful."
   Stand in front of a mirror with your hand on your heart and say out loud:
   "I deserve to be happy, healthy and successful."

Purpose

Purpose is the aim or goal towards which you strive. Living with purpose means that you live with determination and resolve to reach your goals. When you consciously live with purpose, you will be more focused and productive.

Exercise 2.10 What is my purpose?
Ask yourself the following questions. Write freely with no self judgment. If you struggle to come up with ideas, take some time to think and come back to it.
   So what is my life all about?

- What is the purpose of my life?
- What does my life mean?
- What is my reason for living?
- Am I living my life with purpose, right now?
- How can I live with more purpose?

Don't worry if there is some duplication in your answers.

Avoiding regret

It saddens me to hear people talking of regret. The "would have," "could have," "should have" conversations that people have, all too often. Examples include: "I would have gone back to work but I'm so out of touch, no one would want me", "I could have gone to that seminar, if only I could have found childcare." Or "I should have kept up my skills while I was at home with the kids".

Palliative care nurse Bonnie Ware produced a most fascinating list of the "regrets of the dying". Here are the top five:

1. "I wish I'd had the courage to live a life true to myself, not the life others expected of me."
   This is, of course, shows the importance of living true to your authentic self.
2. "I wish I didn't work so hard."
   This regret occurs when we live our life without being true to what we value. Of course, work is very necessary from a financial perspective but it is tricky to get the work-life balance right. By being clear about your values, you can protect yourself from this future regret.
3. "I wish I'd had the courage to express my feelings."
   Again, this regret arises from repressing your authentic self and not letting it have a courageous voice. So let that inner voice sing!
4. "I wish I had stayed in touch with my friends."
   Connection and love are essential human needs but often we overlook them when life is very busy. You can't keep in touch with everyone you ever meet, but important relationships and friendships are worth some time and energy (see Chapter 8).

5. "I wish that I had let myself be happier."
    Imagine realizing on your deathbed that all you needed to be happy had been with you your whole life. Happiness is a choice. It is about contentment with what you have. It is about living with purpose and passion. It is about stopping to notice the good things in life and embracing them.

Exercise 2.11 Regrets

Answer the following questions:

- What regrets do I have now?
- What regrets do I want to avoid having on my deathbed?
- What am I doing to avoid these regrets?

Your thoughts

The types of thought patterns you have are hard-wired into your brain. Many habits, beliefs, attitudes and memories are stored in subconscious mind. Some are positive and serve you well. Others are harmful and hold you back, from living your dream life. Your thoughts are affected by your genetics, past experiences, environment and brain health. In Chapter 4, you will learn more about regulating your thoughts. For now, we will consider a one particular type of positive thought: your aspirations, those conscious thoughts you have about the life you'd love to be living.

Most of us have fleeting thoughts such as "I'd like that dress", "it would be fun to learn to dance," or "it would be nice to be slim again." These thoughts may enter your consciousness briefly but then slip away. But when you focus on an aspirational thought and repeat it over and over, your brain will thoroughly process this information, and you are more likely to take action to make your dream a reality.

Exercise 2.12 Aspirations

This is a brainstorming exercise. Consider each question, and then write freely, without judgment:

- If money was no option how would I live my life?
- What would my perfect life be like in five years time?
- Which of my aspirations or dreams are unfulfilled?
- What desires do I have for my future?
- What aspirations do I have for my family?

In the chapters that follow you will become clear about your aspirations. You will begin to make plans on how to reach them, and how to get your body and mind in a peak state to maximize your chances of achieving your dream life.

In this last exercise of Chapter Two, you will summarize what you have learned about yourself.

Exercise 2.12 Fabulous ME!
Summarize what you have learned in this chapter. Be honest yet concise. Treat this page with ultimate respect and review it often. Share it if you wish, but only with people you trust.

- My story
- My values (top three)
- My strengths (top few)
- My passions
- My needs
- My purpose
- My aspirations

Struggling to find the authentic self

The exercises in this chapter are just the beginning of your lifelong journey of connecting with your authentic self. There are many routes to further develop your authentic self: courses, religion, mediation, coaching and therapy, to name just a few. For some of us, this journey to better know our authentic self can seem a struggle. According to Deepak Chopra in The Shadow Effect, there are many reasons why it may be difficult: excessive stress, emotional pressures, distractions, depression and anxiety, lack of discipline or commitment and opposing intentions. Be patient and gentle with yourself and celebrate the progress you make. If one route is not working for you, look for another. Most of all never stop trying.

The next step

I hope this chapter has helped you better understand your authentic self and begin to create a vision for your future life. The next stage is to take positive action. Chapter 3 will help you design a rock solid plan to achieve fast, effective, lasting change.

Chapter 2 Summary

Your authentic self is who you really are. Gaining a better understanding of your authentic self will help you design your life to increase your happiness, health, wellbeing and success.

There are many facets to "authentic self." These include your:

- personal perspective on your story
- values
- strengths and weaknesses
- passions
- needs
- purpose
- thought patterns, including aspirations

If you live your life true to your authentic self, you will be able to move towards the life you dream of and deserve.

Meeting your own needs is not selfish; it is essential. For only then, will you be able to meet the needs of the people you love.

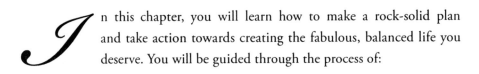

Chapter 3

℘ **PLAN TO SUCCEED** ℘

*I*n this chapter, you will learn how to make a rock-solid plan and take action towards creating the fabulous, balanced life you deserve. You will be guided through the process of:

- Designing a clear plan
- Getting motivated
- Overcoming procrastination
- Getting unblocked
- Creating accountability.

Writing a plan

Writing a detailed, clear action plan helps turn an idea into a goal, increases productivity and motivation and reduces procrastination. The process of writing down your goals and plans activates neural circuits in the visual and kinesthetic areas of your brain. Saying your thoughts out loud will also activate the auditory areas, and you will further increase your chances of success.

My plan

After two years of staying at home full time, I hit a wall of boredom and frustration. I missed working, being part of a team, contributing to a bigger cause and most of all learning. So I decided to enroll in a course, as returning to medicine was not an option at the time. I had so many ideas: one day I was going to be a plumber (yes, really, I had watched a TV show about women plumbers), the next day a counselor, and the next day an interior designer. I spent my days researching my "latest idea", and then would stand in the shower the following morning and come up with my new "latest idea." It was exhausting, overwhelming and confusing. Then one day I got angry with myself for my indecision. I sat and thought about why I was failing to decide and came to the conclusion that I needed a plan.

I thought back to how productive I had been as a public health doctor. In this role, my largest project was "investigating the rise in patients presenting to the Emergency Room." At first, the project felt huge and overwhelming. I had to analyze a database of hundreds of thousands of records, and this was in 1996, when computers that could handle this kind of data were the size of houses. My mentor at the time knew I had lots of good ideas, but that I also could be a bit scattered. He sat me down and made me write an extremely detailed plan. Together, we broke the project down into many small steps; each with a deadline. He asked me to report back weekly on my progress, so we could review and adapt the plan.

Within three months, I had turned this overwhelming project into a finished piece of work, and my recommendations were being implemented by the health authority. It was a great feeling!

Now back to my life of tidying toys, scrubbing toilets, wiping noses and the occasional chat over coffee with a friend. I thought to myself, "My life is important to me. I deserve to make it better. I need a really good plan."

I had just started reading "Be your own life coach", by Fiona Harrold. With the help of this book, I developed a "Personal Plan". For the first time in a long time, I felt clear about what I wanted and why. I came up with a schedule for research with a two-week deadline to make my decision. I recruited "my team" of advisors: my husband and a good friend. Two weeks later, research done, I committed to training to be a counselor.

It felt great to make the decision. With that accomplished, I moved to the next step of my plan and enrolled in a two year counseling course.

I enjoyed the training but had a nagging voice telling me that this model of "therapy" didn't suit me. I enjoyed giving counseling but dreaded receiving it. For me, it felt like too much navel gazing and dwelling on the past. I was crying out for a more future-facing model and discovered Life Coaching. I began the whole planning process again, safe in the knowledge that the previous two years had taught me a lot. Without my plan, who knows what I would have done; maybe I would be a plumber!

So ask yourself: "Do I deserve a better life, with more health, happiness and success?" If the answer is "YES" then you NEED a really good plan.

My model for personal transformation has morphed over the years, drawing on my experience and constant learning as a physician and coach. I use it regularly in my own life, every time I feel stuck and it always helps me gain clarity, focus and momentum.

The Personal Development Plan

This is a process for when:

- You want to make a significant change in your life,
- The change you want to make is complex, or
- You are struggling to move forward.

The process is a little time consuming, but there is a good reason for each step. If you take the time to do it, I promise you will get that time back several times over due to improved focus and productivity. It may even save you money in the long term, as making the wrong decision can be costly.

Exercise 3.1 Personal Development Plan

Promise to be honest with yourself. This process is to help YOU improve YOUR life.

Complete your plan in one sitting, with full attention and no distractions.

Personal Development Process

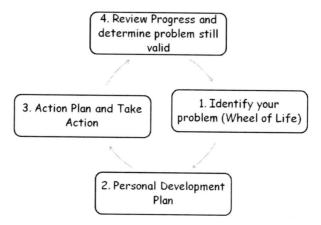

Ask yourself the following questions:

1. What is my problem? It might be:
   - A practical problem, like deciding what course to take or finding a tutor for your child,
   - A life asset that you want to improve (exercise 2.2 "Wheel of Life") OR
   - A weakness that you would like to overcome, such as being disorganized.
2. Why do I want to solve this problem? List all of the reasons without judging them.
3. What is my desired outcome? And how close am I to the desired outcome?
4. What are the consequences of NOT changing? Consider this question in terms of now, in five years and in ten years time.
5. What will I miss out on if I don't change?
6. Have I ever achieved this outcome before? If the answer is "yes," then also ask: What was different in my life then? And what worked then?
7. What are ALL of my possible options? For this question, close your eyes for a few minutes and think about all of the ideas you have for changing this area of your life. Don't over think it; let the ideas flow. When you

have run out of ideas, open your eyes and write down every one of them. Do not criticise any idea.

8. Do I have any beliefs about this area of my life that are holding me back? For example, you might think "no-one in my family has ever been wealthy" or "my brain isn't up to going back to work." We will deal with these negative beliefs in Chapter 4.

9. What's stopping me from reaching my outcome? This may be a problem with self-confidence, time-management or child care.

10. What are my goals?

Smart people set S.M.A.R.T. goals:

- **S**pecific: be very clear about what you want to achieve.
- **M**easurable: use a numerical value if possible.
- **A**chievable and **R**ealistic: be sensible. Think about what is practical for you, given your current situation. It is better to set small goals and review often, than to set a big goal you simply can't achieve. You can always set the bar higher next time.
- **T**imetabled: schedule a time by which you want to achieve your goal.

Here's an example of a NOT-SMART goal: I want to get a job and earn some money in the next month and pay off all my debts.

The S.M.A.R.T. alternative might be: in the next six weeks, I will get a job earning $20 per hour with the aim of paying off all of my debts within the next six months.

11. What will help motivate me? For example you might want to lose weight because your school reunion is approaching.

12. Who will be my Team? The people in your team must be trustworthy and have your best interests in mind. If you need unbiased advice, consider getting a coach.

13. How will I reward myself when I have achieved my goals? Just like kids collecting gold stars, sometimes adults need extra motivation. Rewards needn't cost any money, but they must be things you will look forward

to. You may find that accomplishing your goal is enough of motivation for you. If so, go for it!

Chunking

A large goal, like losing 20lbs or returning to work, can seem overwhelming and paralyze your efforts. The answer is to break the large goals into multiple mini goals. These should be realistic, yet challenging. The next exercise will help you do this.

Exercise 3.2 Action Timeline

Draw a horizontal line on a page in your journal or workbook. Mark the far left of the line NOW and the far right OUTCOME.

Close your eyes and imagine that six months have passed and you have achieved your outcome. You are feeling very proud of yourself. How will your life be different and how you will feel? Now imagine you are travelling back from the OUTCOME, think about all of the things you had to do in order to achieve your outcome. Think about all of the stages of the process. Open your eyes and write down your ideas on your timeline with dates for achieving each goal.

Action Plan and Taking Action

Now that you have clearly identified the details of your plan, it is time for action. Without action, the plan is useless.

Exercise 3.3 Action Plan

Complete the exercise from the workbook or create a table with four columns. Column 1 = action, 2 = priority, 3 = Date, 4 = done. The Action Plan is your to-do-list of specific tasks due for completion, by a specified date.

For example:

- *Enroll in web design class at library. Date: By 27th*
- *Book an appointment with college advisor. Date: By 12th*
- *Schedule a date night. Date: Today*

Next prioritize the actions. 1 = urgent do today, through to 5 = non urgent, it can wait.

Begin priority 1's right away: there is no time like the present. Enter a date, by which you would like to accomplish the task. When you complete an action, put a check in column 4. It feels good to complete a task and may inspire you to do more.

Reviewing your progress

After a period of time, you are going to review your progress and determine the next steps.

Exercise 3.4 Review Progress

Print the exercise from the workbook or create a table with four columns. Column 1 = action, 2 = level of success, 3 = reasons, 4 = learning.

Step 1. Refer back to your Action Plan. Write out all of the actions.

Step 1. What was your level of success? 10 = successfully completed action by due date, 0 = did nothing. Consider the reasons for your level of success. Be honest.

Step 1. Ask yourself:
- What did I learn?
- What would I do differently next time?

Sometimes after a period of action, you realize "I don't desire this outcome any longer." This is fine, as long as you are sure. Learn from the process and don't waste any more time on it. Be clear about why you no longer desire the outcome and then move on, no regrets.

If you have completely achieved your goals and the problem is solved, go wild and celebrate with your promised reward. Consider if there is another life asset, problem or weakness you might like to focus on next. If you still have more work to do, review or repeat the Personal Development Plan and start the process again.

A whole life approach

You may have several areas of your life that you want to work on at one time, and this is okay, as long as you don't overwhelm yourself and become ineffective. Complete the process above for any major changes you desire. You may want to combine action plans and prioritize urgent actions.

When your plan is not working

For most people, this process will work well. In a short time, they will be making positive progress towards their goals. Occasionally people have a good plan but still don't succeed, due to inappropriate action, lack of persistence or the goal not working out the way they hoped. If this applies to you, do not be discouraged. Focus on figuring out why and adapting your plan accordingly.

The reasons for lack of progress usually lies in one of the three stages of the ASPIRE model. So here's what to do:

- Review the facets of your authentic self. Ask "is what I am doing conflicting with my authentic self?" Ask your authentic self for guidance.
- Start the Personal Development Plan from scratch. Consider focusing on one area of change at a time until you are making good progress. Be sure you still want to achieve your outcome.
- Ensure that you are in a good emotional and physical state. Chapters 4, 6 and 8 will help you with this.
- Lastly, consider another model of change, like a personal development course, a retreat or one-to-one coaching.

Julie's Plan

- *What is my problem?*
  I am unhealthy. I'm afraid I am going to get diabetes.
- *Why do I want to solve this problem?*
  I want to live a long healthy life. I hate being sick or in pain. I want to have the energy to enjoy life and have fun with my children. I want to be able to travel when the kids leave home. I want to have a long, happy retirement with my husband.

- *What is my desired outcome? How close am I to the desired outcome?*

     Get down to 120lbs. Be able to run a 5k. Have a healthy relationship with food.

     I am 150lbs. I can't run 1k. I eat too much junk food and not enough fresh food.

- *What are the consequences of NOT changing? (Now, in five years and in ten years)*

     Now: I feel tired all the time. I feel bad about the way I look. I constantly regret my food decisions.

     Five years: I will probably have diabetes or cancer. I will be more unfit and fatter.

     10 years: OMG I am going to be so unhealthy. How will I be able to enjoy life and keep up with my kids and my husband? I am really going to regret this if I don't change.

- *What will I miss out on if I don't change?*

     I'm going to miss out on vacations, having fun and being a happy, healthy old lady.

- *Have I ever achieved this outcome before? What was different in my life then? What worked then?*

     I was quite fit and ate well when I was in my late twenties. This was before children. Back then I had more time and discipline, and I kept no junk food in the house. I exercised on my way to work. I ate salad or soup for lunch.

- *What are ALL of my possible options?*

     Work with my coach. Commit to exercising daily. Get my family to help me. Stop buying junk food: the kids can have it occasionally when we are out. Enrol in class at gym. Get hypnotized. Get friend to commit with me.

- *Do I have any beliefs about this area of my life that are holding me back?*

     Several family members have diabetes: it's inevitable I'll get it. I'll always be overweight. I'm not strong enough to change.

- *What's stopping me from reaching my outcome?*

ME! Not scheduling time. Buying junk food. Not prioritizing. If I am half hearted about changing, I slip back quickly. I need to make a radical change and I need to do it NOW.

- *What are my goals?*

    Exercise daily: 20 minutes on work days, 45 on days off. I will do this for six weeks, then I will run a 5K.

    Change my diet: Have a green drink for breakfast. Salad for lunch. Healthy meal for dinner.

- *What will help motivate me?*

    Getting fit. I'm taking responsibility, for my life. Only I can change myself. Besides, the alternative is just too terrifying. I'm going to explain to my family why I want to change and ask for their help. Organizing the 5K will motivate me. Having my coach as an accountability partner, will help.

- *Who will be my Team?*

    My husband, my kids, my health coach and my fit friends.

- *How will I reward myself when I have achieved my goals?*

    After running the 5K, I'll have a massage.

    When I reach 120lbs, I'll buy new clothes. I'm going to need them!

    Achieving my goals is going to be really rewarding. I want this, I need this, and so I'm going to make it happen.

Action Plan and Review

- *Action 1: Sign up for 5k*

    Priority: 1 = Urgent

    Date: Today

    Level of success: Ten. Did it straight away

    Reasons: I didn't wait

    Learning: If I don't give myself time to procrastinate, I get things done

- *Action 2: Book six weeks of appointments with my health coach*

    Priority: 2

    Date: Within three days

Level of success: 5: I did it in five days

Reason: I kept forgetting to email for appointments.

Learning: I should have done it right away.

- *Action 3: Sign up for weekly pilates class with friend*

    Priority: 2

    Date: Tomorrow (when at gym)

    Level of success: Four

    Reason: I signed up as planned. Then I got a cold, son was ill and I missed two classes; still, I did two classes in the month.

    Learning: Life gets in the way sometimes! I really enjoyed the classes. Keep trying.

Chapter 3 Summary

A well-thought-out, well-executed plan will help you turn your dreams into reality.

Step 1. Connect with your authentic self

Step 2. Clearly identify:

- Your problem
- Your desired outcome
- The consequences of inaction
- Barriers to change
- Your motivators
- Your team
- Your rewards
- Set S.M.A.R.T. Goals: Specific, Measurable, Achievable, Realistic and Timetabled.
- Chunk large goals into mini goals

Step 3. Write an action plan

Step 4. TAKE ACTION

Step 5. Review Progress

Consider a whole life approach or focus on one problem at a time

If your strategy is not working, do not be defeated. Get determined and figure out why it is not working. It's up to you to make it work.

Chapter 4

℘ PEAK PERFORMANCE ℘

"℘eak performance training" is used by people from many walks of life: athletes, actors, singers, top business people and soldiers and is in essence, "self-regulation" training. Moms, dads, children and especially teens and young adults taking exams can likewise benefit. What's more, it's not as daunting as it sounds.

Self-regulation

In this chapter, you will learn the art of self-regulation. Self-regulation is the ability to control the "state" of your body and mind, in a variety of situations, so that you can achieve your goals in record time. For example, if you are about to go for a run, you want to feel energetic and positive, however, if you are about to go into your first job interview in ten years, you might want to be calm, alert and focused.

Many of us spend much of our time in the wrong state. We feel stressed when we should be calm, wide awake when we should be asleep or sad when we should be happy.

We humans have a remarkable ability to regulate our state, but many of us don't know how. Did you know you can consciously change the rhythm of your heart and your brainwaves just by breathing and thinking differently? People have been regulating their state for peak performance for thousands of years. They have mastered this art of regulation through contemplative practice, such as meditation and prayer, and through disciplines such as yoga and martial arts. Recent research has proven that these and other self-regulation techniques can alter individual performance and even the very function of the body and brain.

I have practiced self-regulation for several years now and have taught it to many people, including kindergarten students with autism. If they can learn it, so can you. When mastered, it can be like a magic wand, which you wave, to choose your state, for any situation. Rather like learning martial arts, mastery of self-regulation is a life-long journey; it takes effort and determination, but I promise you it is worth it.

Your state is determined by three things:

- Physiology: Health of your body. Often described in terms of how well you feel, your energy levels and the presence or absence of symptoms and illness.
- Psychology: Health of your mind. Often described in terms of contentment, calmness, thought patterns, feeling in control or balanced or by the diagnosis of a developmental or mental health problem.
- Focus: What your mind is focusing on. Often described in terms of attention, engagement, motivation or the ability to control impulses.

Examples:

Susan is an intelligent, caring mom. She is focusing on reading a book for her book club. One day she is fit and well, and so she sits and reads for two hours, fully understanding and enjoying the book. The next day she has a head cold. Her body aches and she has a terrible headache. She reads for five minutes, before realizing, she has not been paying attention and can't remember a word she has read. Two very different experiences of reading a book: One productive, the other not. The difference? Her physiology.

Alice is training for a 10K run. She is in a great mood. She goes to the gym and does a great workout, returning home to get on with her day. She feels motivated and energized. The next morning, she wakes early; worrying about a bill she has just received. She goes through her bank statements and feels very anxious. Reluctantly, she drags herself to the gym. Once she gets there, her mind is not on the workout. She is clumsy and distracted, and strains her calf, because she didn't stretch. Two very different experiences of training: One successful, the other not. The difference? Her psychology.

Katy has decided to take a course to further her career. She starts her day by checking her to-do-list, writing a daily schedule and researching courses. She has a productive day and makes a short list. The next day she starts her day checking social media, and gets caught up in a discussion with friends and reading news online. Before she knows it, it is past lunchtime and the kids are coming home soon. She gives up on researching that day but feels frustrated with her lack of progress. Two very different days: One productive, the other not. The difference? Her focus.

Optimizing state

State is hard to measure and describe as it is highly dependent on personal perspective. Like happiness, there is no numerical value for state. People don't wander round saying "I'm in a 100 percent peak state today!" Self-regulation and peak performance techniques simply optimize your current state, so that you can do your best in any situation. This empowers you and improves your productivity, efficiency, accuracy and success.

Characteristics of Peak Performance state:

When you are in a peak state you might feel:

- Physically well (pain and symptom free)
- Energetic
- Content
- Calm
- Able to control impulses
- Motivated
- Focused
- Positive
- In control and balanced

Your state

In any moment, we may describe our state by the prominent feeling at the time.

Examples:

If you have flu, you are most aware of your physiology, so describe yourself as being "tired and achy."

If you are feeling sad and hopeless, you are most aware of your psychology, so would describe yourself as feeling "depressed."

If you have a million things to do and don't know where to start, you are most aware of your focus, so would describe yourself as "distracted and overwhelmed."

My clients are often intrigued to learn that they can have control over their future state.

The next exercise will help you evaluate your current, past and desired state.

Exercise 4.1 I gotta feeling!

Put your hand on your heart and connect with your authentic self. Take three deep breaths before reading each statement out loud, and then write down your answers:

- Right now I am feeling…
- In the past week, I have felt…
- I'm tired of feeling... (call this Z)
- I feel Z when…(describe the things that make you feel this way)
- What is the opposite of Z? (call this A)
- I feel A when…
- I want to feel… (M)
- I feel M when…
- Ideas on how I can feel less Z…
- Ideas on how I can feel more A…
- Ideas on how I can feel more M…

Did you see a pattern or theme? I know I do whenever I complete this exercise.

Julie's "I gotta feeling"

When Julie first came to see me, she was not in a good state. Here are her responses:

Right now I am feeling: Confused, frustrated, unhappy and overwhelmed.

In the past week I have felt: All of the above, plus exhausted, sad, and like a failure.

I'm tired of feeling (call this Z): All of the above; I am also tired of feeling that I don't contribute financially to my family and that I am inefficient.

I feel Z when: I am paying more for childcare than I am earning, working long hours and having to do most of the housework. I feel that returning to work was the wrong decision. I feel like I am doing my best but it's just not working.

What is the opposite of Z (A): Happy, relaxed, energetic, clear, focused and successful.

I feel A when I am working and it's all going well, when I am doing something fun with my family, when I work out, when I am clear about my work future, and when I listen to relaxation CDs.

I want to feel (M): Happy, energetic, in control, focused, financially productive, fun, and close to my husband.

I feel M when I am with my family, when my job is going well, and when I take a night out with husband or friends.

Ideas on how I can feel less Z: I need to find balance between work and home, and a job that I can manage better; I need to get my family to help around the house.

Ideas on how I can feel more A: Work out three times a week, find the right job, plan more fun activities with my family, and listen to relaxation CD before the start of day.

Ideas on how I can feel more M: Exercise often, find the right job, plan date nights with my husband, and plan fun activities with family and friends.

Physiology

Your physical health and in particular your brain health, is the key to happiness, wellbeing and success. Poor physical health will reduce the ability of your brain and mind to function optimally. Any impairment of brain function may cause problems with performing tasks, making good decisions and taking positive, planned action.

Think of health as being like your finances, you have assets and liabilities. The key to improving health is increasing your health assets and decreasing your health liabilities.

Self-regulation is about learning to listen to your body and discover what works for you. Your body is unique and will respond in its own way to lifestyle change, interventions or treatments. If an intervention makes you feel energetic and relieves symptoms, then it's probably good for you. If an intervention leaves you feeling sick, tired and achy, then it's probably bad for you. As a physician, I always told my patients "listen to your body."

I urge you to try natural or side-effect-free solutions first, for any minor health problem. For example, if you have a headache, try drinking more water, diaphragmatic breathing and resting with your eyes shut for ten minutes, instead of popping a pill. It may work just as quickly as a pill and has no side effects. It always amazes me how many people would rather try medications with a long list of side effects, than make simple lifestyle changes.

If you have major health problems, it is essential that you seek expert advice. But I recommend that you become a well-informed patient: Do some research and make a list of questions to ask. Note their answers. Ask for a comprehensive list of treatment options, with pros and cons for each, so that you can make the right decision, for you.

In Chapter 6, we will address physical health in much greater detail.

Psychology

Psychology refers to your state of mind. Your psychological health can be suboptimal without causing a significant problem, such as depression or anxiety. The good news is that you can always do things to improve or stabilize the function of your mind.

According to Dan Siegel and the consensus of his team of experts "*the mind is an embodied and relational process that regulates energy and information flow*". In other words, the mind is the flow of chemical and electrical signals within the brain. These signals relate to information to and from sources external to our body (including interactions with other people) and internal within our body and the brain itself. The function of our mind affects our thoughts, feelings, memories, attitudes, beliefs, dreams, ideas and actions.

In Chapter 8, we will discuss the health of your mind further, with topics including thought patterns, stress and habits.

Focus

Focus is sustained mental attention on a task. For me, focus has been my biggest challenge since becoming a mom. Why can't I find my son's soccer boots? Because I am not sustaining focus for long enough to find them. Why did I forget to make that dentist appointment? Because I didn't focus on the thought of making the appointment, for long enough to make it happen.

From a brain perspective, focus requires your brain's conscious engagement, in one main task at a time. The more focused you are in any task, the more efficient you will be. If you are not focused, you will be inefficient and make errors. If a job is worth doing, it is worth doing with focus.

I have worked with hundreds of people with ADHD and ADD, and their main challenge is lack of focus. One ADHD client told me that, he sometimes felt like he was watching 20 TV's, each showing a different show. No wonder he felt constantly distracted and unable to follow any one storyline in his life!

ADHD and ADD are Neurodevelopmental disorders characterized by problems with attention, focus and impulsivity and in some cases, hyperactivity (of thoughts or movement); that's the H in ADHD. Many adults tell me "I think I have ADHD." Well, unless they had significant problems in these areas before the age of seven, it is not ADHD. What they may have is a problem with the function of their "frontal lobe": The region of the brain that acts as its CEO. These problems can occur in adults due to injury, illness, chronic stress and possibly even the overuse of electronic devices. Symptoms include problems planning, executive function deficiencies, short term memory problems, mood instability and impulsiveness.

If you have significant problems with focus, see your doctor, for advice on whether you need investigations.

Most people can improve their ability to focus by practicing tasks which require sustained focus (duh, I know it sounds obvious).

Flow

Flow is the highest level of engagement, of focused motivation. When was the last time you were so engrossed in something you lost track of time? When you are "in flow", you feel positive, energized and aligned with the task. "Flow state" is good for your brain and body. Sadly, many busy moms rarely achieve flow because life is just too hectic. Getting into a flow state can take time and can be easily disrupted.

I recently went kayaking with my husband, just the two of us. I am novice kayaker, so initially I had to focus intently on not tipping over and steering in the right direction. Soon I was "in the flow." It was a lovely warm day. As I got into the rhythm of paddling, I forgot everything; I felt like I was at one with the kayak. I remained in this flow state for several minutes, moving gently through the water, being vaguely aware of my husband, the sea and the world around me. It felt really good. Then a nearby boat revved its engine and "boom" I was back in the real world. I was still enjoying the moment, but now new thoughts crept into my mind such as worries about my children and my long to-do-list.

Exercise 4.3 In the Flow

In your journal, make a note of all the times you can remember being in flow.

- What were you doing? How did you feel?
- Is there a pattern?
- Is there something that you could do today so that you could experience flow?

Self-regulation Toolkit

Self-regulation is all about what works for you. By developing your own toolkit and using the tools when needed, you will have more control over your life.

Here are some ideas of things that might put you into a peak performance state. The list that follows is by no means exhaustive and your own ideas may be more powerful:

- Lifestyle
  Increase: Nutrition, hydration, exercise routine, sleep and healthy habits.

Decrease: Intake of harmful foods and substances (such as tobacco and alcohol), risk of injury and activities or people that cause you stress.

- Build positive relationships
  Spending time with people who make you feel good is a precious source of renewal. Accept help from these people when you are in need: Doing so will serve you well and it will make them feel good too. Win-win!
- Engage in activities that put you in a positive state
  Choose activities that make you laugh or feel energetic, excited, happy, focused, or relaxed. Don't let anyone else tell you what you enjoy. For example, there are many people who find massage relaxing but many who do not. Likewise, there are people who find zip-lining fun, and many others find it terrifying.
- Journaling
  Journaling can be an excellent way to improve self-regulation. Wire your brain for success by writing about your health, life goals, positive thoughts and emotions and lessons learned.
- Diaphragmatic breathing
  Diaphragmatic breathing takes only a couple of minutes and increases the amount of oxygen you inhale and calms your nervous system.
  Instructions: Put your hand on your tummy. With the next breath out, blow out all the air from your lungs. As you breathe back in, notice your tummy move out. As you breathe out, notice your tummy move in. Repeat for a couple of minutes. If you feel dizzy, stop.
- Meditation, relaxation, mindfulness and prayer
  There is powerful evidence that these can improve the health of mind and body. Consistency and practice are important to reap the benefits of these practices.
  Meditation can be used alone, or as part of religious practice. If you are one of the many people, who struggle to learn meditation alone, try a class or online training. I offer a free 14 day program, of five minute meditations: visit www.beyondsoccermom.com, to try it out.
- Biofeedback
  Biofeedback techniques increase awareness and control of physiological functions and can help improve focus and psychology. Tools range from

a one dollar mood ring, controlled by finger temperature, to the highly complex technology of heart-rhythm biofeedback and Neurofeedback (brain waves). For people with significant conditions such as ADHD and migraine, professionally led biofeedback can be a valuable adjunct to traditional treatment.

Exercise 4.4 Self-regulation Toolkit

Step 1. Make a list of things that make you feel:
- Healthy
- Energetic
- Content
- Calm
- In control of your life
- In control of your impulses
- Balanced
- Positive
- Focused
- Motivated
- Productive and successful

Step 2. Make a list of:
- Lifestyle changes you need to make
- People who make you feel good
- Activities that put you in a positive state
- Other techniques that might improve your state

Changing state or "the art of self-regulation"

Self-regulation can be learned by almost anyone. It begins with a conscious decision to change, and six simple steps:

Step 1. Identify the problem

Step 2. Identify desired outcome

Step 3. Observe current state

Step 4. Compare current state to desired outcome

Step 5. Practice new state or behavior

Step 6. Monitor progress. Go back to step one if necessary.

The following exercise will help you plan to improve self-regulation and enhance your state.

Exercise 4.5 Peak Performance Plan

Step 1. Complete Exercise 3.1 "Personal Development Plan" for changing your state. Question 1 is "What is the problem with my state?" The problem might be the frequency of negative thinking, energy levels, contentment, control, balance, focus, motivation, or stress.

Step 2. Complete action plan. Exercise 3.3.

Step 3. TAKE ACTION.

Step 4. Review progress. See Exercise 3.4.

Gaining mastery

So now you have started your journey to becoming a peak performing mom! It's a lifelong journey, so be patient and kind to yourself. The goal is improvement and progress, and as with any new skill, this takes time.

Julie's State

When we started to work on improving Julie's state, we began with developing a daily mantra to help her focus on her goals and get into a positive frame of thinking. She repeated the mantra daily for one month and still uses it today. She found it quickly helped her get laser-focused on her goals and avoid procrastination.

Julie felt she sometimes got into a flow state at work and when she was walking in the woods near her home, with her dog. She realized how powerful and therapeutic this simple daily "chore" was for her.

Exercise 4.4 helped Julie discover that her toolkit needed to include: Regular exercise, drinking a green smoothie for breakfast, working part-time, walking her dog, saying a daily mantra, avoiding social media in the morning, having a detailed action plan and reviewing it daily. She also identified a small group of friends and family who were trustworthy and supportive. In our sessions, I taught Julie meditation, which at first she found difficult because her mind was very active. Within a month, of daily practice and journaling, meditation had become a powerful stress-reliever for Julie.

Exercise 4.5 focused on Julie feeling exhausted, negative, dissatisfied and overwhelmed; and revealed that she was eating emotionally and feeling like a failure in many aspects of her life. Julie knew she needed to change her state and that life would be much better when she did. She was convinced that if she didn't change that she was going to get a chronic illness, like diabetes. She hadn't felt in a good state since becoming a parent. She believed that stress and chronic illness were her destiny, but was very happy to let go of these false beliefs. She knew that what was stopping her was her inability to filter out distractions and setting unrealistic goals. So her goals for improving state were:

Daily five minute meditation, repetition of mantra and journal keeping for one month

Green smoothie for breakfast, immediate action

Exercise three times a week for one month.

To meet all of her goals, she enlisted the help of her husband and a good friend who agreed to keep her accountable. She did not need any reward; her goals were enough.

Chapter 4 Summary

When we learn to self regulate our "state," we can achieve better results in less time.

State has three major components:

- Physiology
- Psychology
- Focus

When we learn to optimize all three components, we can learn to get into a "Peak State."

Improving focus takes practice. When in a focused state we get things done more quickly and efficiently. The state of "flow" is the ultimate focused state.

The key to Peak Performance is identifying and using your unique Self-regulation Toolkit.

PART TWO

Chapter 5

⤳ TIME ⤳

*T*ime is precious! You can't get it back when it's gone. Not many people at the end of their days wishing they had spent more time doing housework, checking email or playing games on Facebook. Most people say they wish they had spent more time with their family, having fun, achieving and contributing more. So, if you want to create the fabulous balanced life you desire and deserve, you will benefit from learning how to spend your time wisely.

Now if you are a well organized mom, who never has a to-do-list longer than a few items, then the rest of this chapter may not have much to offer you.

If you are one of those moms, like me, who marvels at how some super-moms, seem to have more hours in their day than you; this chapter is for you. Surely those super-moms rarely sleep or eat; they must have an army of staff working for them or maybe they have magic powers over time? The truth is that they are probably just more organized and better at managing their time than you and me.

I have to admit that, while I have read many books and taken courses on time management, it still remains a great challenge for me as a mother. I find it hard to prioritize important tasks if they are boring, and I frequently get distracted by "shiny objects," such as a new book or TV show, which are much more interesting to me than housework. I have, however, learned to be more efficient. When I decided to write this book, I challenged myself to become more time efficient. I researched and drew together everything I knew on time management and then pulled out the best bits. I am about to share with you the gems that I feel confident will work for busy moms. I used the strategies you are about to learn to ensure I got the first draft of this book written in two months (which was realistic for me) and to stay on top of managing my home and family. I admit there have been times when my children ran out of clean socks because I hadn't put the laundry away, but we all survived!

The Ten Step Plan for Managing Your Time

Step One: Take Stock
Complete exercise 3.1 "Personal Development Plan" with "time management" or "organizational skills" as the answer to question 1, "What is my problem?"

Exercise 5.1 Time Audit
Step 1. Print the exercise from the workbook or take notes in your journal.

Step 2. From the moment, you get up, time and log everything you do that takes more than five minutes.

Step 3. At the end of the day, categorize how you spent your time. The worksheet, categorizes activities common to most moms, add in any that are unique to you. Total up the time for each activity category. If you are not using the worksheet, devise categories such as "housework" and "driving"

Step 4. Give each activity category a score for:
- Priority value or importance: A score of 0 means that not doing the activity would have no consequences; a score of 5 means that leaving an activity undone would have resulted in significant consequences.
- Satisfaction value for you: A score of 0 means "I hated every moment of this" a score of 5 means "I loved every moment."
- Family value: 0 = no value; 5 = extremely valuable

- Financial value: Score by including the money you saved by doing this and the money you earned. 0 = no value; 5 = high value.
- Total value (optional): A total value might not be appropriate in all activities.

Step 5. Now compare the total time and the value for each activity: What do you notice? If you find you are spending lots of time doing tasks which have very little value, then you are not using your time optimally. By noticing those things that you that have little value to you, you can make a conscious decision to drop these tasks or focus on limiting them.

Step 6. Add to your action plan if you are now aware of things you need to do to improve your efficiency. For example: If you realize you spend too much time driving your child to after school activities, you might add "arrange car pool". If you realize you spend too little time with your partner, you might want to plan a monthly date night.

Step Two: The Power of Lists

This step is for moms who are busy and overscheduled. It may seem obsessive, but many of my clients have found this approach to be very useful.

Complete lists 2, 3 and 4 in your own handwriting. This way you will activate the visual and kinesthetic parts of your brain and your mind, and process the information more thoroughly. I sometimes forget to take my to-do-list out with me, but if I close my eyes I can "see" the list in my mind.

List 1: Your calendar

Pick a calendar, of at least 12 months duration, to use consistently. Choose from calendars on your electronic devices or traditional print versions. This is where you write major events like birthdays, vacations and doctor's appointments.

List 2 Monthly Priorities List

At the beginning of every month complete a list of important activities for the month ahead. Keep adding to it. It should include things from your calendar and action plans. Refer back to this list when you are writing your week plan.

Exercise 5.2 Monthly Priorities

At the beginning of every month complete the exercise from the workbook or create a table, with seven columns: Home, family, money, health, social, career and other. Enter any tasks you would like or need to complete this week, for each category.

List 3 Week plan

Once a week write a plan for the coming week. Prioritize the tasks on the to-do-list (Priority 1= urgent and needs to be done today or there will be serious consequences. Priority 5 = not important but it would be nice to do it). Include any events from your calendar, your monthly priority list and your action plan. Add new activities and tasks as they arise and check them off when completed. Putting a big black line through a completed task is satisfying. You might also want to schedule time each week for a major task such as cleaning and laundry.

Exercise 5.3 Week Plan

Complete the exercise in the workbook or create a table, at the beginning of every week. The table should have 4 columns. 1= Day and date, 2 = events, 3 = tasks, 4 = priorities.

List 4: Daily list or "To-do-list"

For this I personally use a post-it note; I put it on my week-plan, on my kitchen counter-top. You might like to use a piece of scrap paper or the Notes app on your phone. Write down in order any events for the day and any tasks you need, or would like to do today. Carry it with you, if you go out. This avoids having one of those days when you think "darn it, I forgot to do X, Y and Z".

List 5: Meal Planner and shopping list (optional)

I have two friends who have worked throughout motherhood. Both are extremely well organized and efficient. Both share a secret to reducing grocery shopping trips to a minimum. Here's what they do: On Saturday they write out a plan for meals for the week ahead. They have a master shopping list, which contains the basics, like milk, bread and cereal, and they add to it ingredients for the meals planned. Then they shop. Occasionally during the week, they make a trip to the grocery store to pick up things they have run out of and fresh produce. They save hours every week by being super efficient with grocery shopping and probably save money too.

Step three: Chunk Big Tasks

Some actions like "setting up a business" or "spring cleaning house" need to be broken down! It is unreasonable to expect to start with a big task like this and keep going until it's finished.

Mary's business

Mary had decided to set up a part-time business, as a mobile hairdresser. She was a great hairdresser but had never worked for herself. When she came to see me she had spent two weeks trying to get the business up and running. She was overwhelmed and was feeling like it was all too much trouble. I explained to her that this was too big a task, to do in one sitting. She needed to break "setting up my business" into manageable chunks and complete them in a sequential order: Business profile and vision (to guide marketing), organization of the business, buying equipment, financial arrangements, marketing and sales and balancing family and work. By doing this, she released the feelings of overwhelm, refocused and got on with the project. Some of the "chunks" took very little time, so she was able to focus time and energy on more important tasks. After two coaching sessions, she had successfully set up the structure of her business and had started work, doing what she did best, making other women look beautiful.

Step four: Beware of distant elephants (or learning to say NO!)

I heard the phrase "beware of distant elephants" several years ago and I love it! Essentially, it means this: An elephant, when far away appears tiny, like a grain of sand. In the same way, big tasks often seem manageable from the distance of several months, so you say agree to do them. As you approach the elephant, or the task, however, you realize it is big – perhaps way too big. If you are not careful, the elephant could crush you, or the task that looked so easy in the distance can suddenly look overwhelming as you near the completion date. I have had the good fortune to ride on the head of an elephant, and I can tell you these metaphoric ones are much more daunting than the real ones.

My elephants

In my second year of being PTA (parent teacher association) Chairperson, I was faced with a distant elephant. I had met this elephant the previous year, when I had volunteered to run the "Christmas Fair" with a friend. The fair was one of the biggest fundraisers, of the year for our small, poorly-funded school. Of the several roles, I took on, one was marketing. In previous years marketing had been minimal, but I had seen other schools doing a much better job. I decided that we needed to get more of the local community to come and so designed and printed a flyer. I asked for volunteers to distribute the 200 flyers, and got a little help. With over a 100 flyers left the day before the fair, I set off in the snow and wind to deliver them. In England, each front door has a "letter-box", for mail delivery, and some of these are wonderfully designed to stop the wind from getting in the house and to trap the knuckles, of whoever is delivering something. After slipping on some black ice three hours into my trudging delivery route, I began to cry. I admitted defeat and took my sore cold knuckles home. The fair made twice the money of the previous year and was great fun, but I had learned my lesson. I had faced this elephant before, and I knew it was big, so I said that I would help co-ordinate and pass on my knowledge, but I did not over commit on this occasion.

The moral of this story is that sometimes you need to say NO! Not just to volunteering but to all of those activities that drain your time and energy, without offering you any real value. If you say NO to reading email every 20 minutes, volunteering for the bake sale when you have an important family event looming, or tidying your kitchen five times a day, you will find you have more time to do valuable tasks.

I am a big fan of volunteering, charity work and contributing to others, and believe it is essential to spiritual growth. However, I also think there is a danger to over-volunteering. You need to be clear about your reasons for volunteering and beware of resentment and burnout.

Step five: Focus and Flow

Focusing on one task, at a time, increases productivity, reduces errors and reduces time on task. If you have an important task to do, it is essential you set aside time to focus on that alone.

If you focus for only short amounts of time on a task, it will take much longer. Each time you lose focus, do something else and then come back to the task you will take considerable time to get back to the level of productivity you were at.

When you actively focus and engage in a task, you may reach a state of "flow". As discussed in Chapter 4, when in flow you are more efficient, accurate and productive.

Step six: Motivate yourself

Motivation fuels your drive and energy. If the task itself is not sufficiently motivating, you might need to build in some extra motivation. Habit based tasks don't require 100 percent of your attention, so you may be able to combine them with another activity. So if you find laundry or cleaning uninspiring, combine it with an enjoyable activity, such watching TV shows on your laptop or listening to music or audio books. I have a playlist on my phone just for housework. They are songs that I can dance to while I am working; I'm sure it makes me slightly less focused on the task, but I enjoy myself and I am thus more likely to do the work. If my neighbors could see me doing housework, they would think I was crazy.

Step seven: Cherish child-free time

Child-free time is an extremely precious resource. Use your child-free time for tasks that require your full focus and attention. During times when you are with your child (with-child time), do tasks that require less focus.

Carole's Story: Finding time to paint

My client Carol repeatedly said she didn't have enough time to paint. When her child was home, she found it very hard to get any painting done. I asked her how she organized her day. It turned out that when her child as at school, she did housework, exercised, contacted friends and then got down to painting, just after lunchtime. This gave her a mere two hours to paint. We came up with a plan: Painting was to become her priority in her child-free-time, along with other more important tasks, like talking to clients. Most other tasks would be done in her with-child-time, like housework and social media. These other tasks might take a bit longer to complete, but they would still get done. By following this simple rule, she found three extra hours a day for her art.

One specific rule that serves me well is that in my child-free time, is that I limit time on email and social media. I get hundreds of emails and notifications each day. During my child-free time, I scan my emails, maybe twice and respond only to urgent messages. Everything else waits until my boys are home and settled. Social media always waits.

Step eight: Limit time on low value tasks

Can you relate to Phyllis Diller's quote: "Cleaning your house while your kids are still growing up is like shoveling the walk before it stops snowing"? The reality of life for most mothers is that they have to do laundry, cooking, shopping and housework. However, these tasks will expand, to take up as much time as you let them. Make a deal with yourself to limit the time on these tasks. One great way to do this is to use a timer, to help you keep track of time. When I am doing chores on a busy day, I time myself. For example I might allow myself 20 minutes to tidy the kitchen. Sometimes I decide I need more time and reset the timer; other times I say "I have done enough for now; I'll do more later".

Step nine: Stay real

Life as a mother is unpredictable and demanding. The reality is that life will sometimes get in the way of your plan: Your child will get sick, school days will be cancelled, and there will be appointments you have to attend. You will need to be flexible and adapt your plan to whatever life throws at you. Sometimes you will have to accept that "now is not the right time" to change your life.

I gave myself eight weeks, to finish the first draft of this book. I planned to write for two to three hours each day. On day seven, Hurricane Sandy hit the North East Coast of America; we had minimal generator power and no internet for six days. We also had a family staying who could not stay in their own home, and my boys were off from school for seven days. I admit, during this time I only wrote for a total of thirty minutes. If it had been urgent, I guess I would have found a way, but I was kind to myself in those extra-ordinary circumstances.

Step ten: Develop habits to save time

It's estimated that more than 60 percent of the things we do every day are habits. Our brain develops habits to save effort. A habit involves little conscious involvement: The neural pathways are so well used that the behavior becomes automatic. The other great thing about habits is that you can often multitask while doing the habit. Research shows that adding one new positive habit will help with develop other new positive habits.

Julie's Time

Julie admitted to becoming increasingly inefficient with her time, in the prior few years. As a teenager and young adult she was well organized, but the increasing demands of motherhood had challenged her skills to breaking point. Julie found the exercises in this chapter very useful for refocusing on what was important. She reviewed her priorities and found that she was able to find more time for herself by restricting time on the computer, arranging car-pooling, using timers for housework, saying "no" to school volunteering (which she had done for years) and only doing housework when the children were home. She made time for regular exercise, meditation and date-night with her partner. She found that she saved 10% on her grocery bill by planning meals and shopping. For the first time, in a long time, she felt in control of her time and energy.

By following some or all of these steps, you should find more time for the tasks that really matter. These steps will not only improve your efficiency and productivity but could save you money and help you improve your health, career and relationships.

Chapter 5 Summary

Increasing your time management skills, will free up time for doing the things that really matter to you.

The Ten Step Plan for Managing Your Time

Step 1: Take stock

Step 2: The Power of Lists

Step 3: Chunk big tasks

Step 4: Learn to say NO

Step 5: Focus and flow

Step 6: Motivate yourself

Step 7: Cherish child-free time

Step 8: Limit time on low-value tasks

Step 9: Stay real

Step 10: Develop habits to save time

Improved efficiency and productivity may also have an added benefit of enhancing all other areas of your wellbeing.

Chapter 6

ᕫᕫ HEALTHY BODY ᕫᕫ

*Y*our health is very precious. When you are well, you may take your health for granted and be complacent. When you do not have good health, it is hard to thrive in any area of your life. When you are sick, you crave good health and to feel energetic.

We live in an age when access to information on health, healthy lifestyle and disease treatment is easy, via the internet. However, for many of us, this information is overwhelming, confusing and contradictory; some of it is untrue and harmful. This chapter aims to introduce you to a simple, yet powerful, model for improving health. This should be used as an adjunct to medical advice and not a replacement. There is more information at www.beyondsoccermom/health for those of you who like more detail.

Ten key facts about health
1. Your body is incredible and complex.
2. Every cell, organ and system in your body is constantly working, co-operating and communicating in order to create balance and healthy function.

3. Good health is a balancing act affected by health assets (things that are good for health) and health liabilities (things that are bad for health).

4. Through your free will, lifestyle choices and behavior, you can influence your health.

5. Optimizing your health will increase wellbeing and success in other areas of your life.

6. Good health will help you be a good mom.

7. By valuing health, you become a great health role model for your children.

8. Being sick comes with significant costs.

9. Health and illness are a spectrum.

10. Your body is sending signals to help you help it to be healthy. When the signals become strong enough, they lead to symptoms such as pain, swelling or fatigue.

Your health and your family

You owe it to your children to be healthy, for then you will be better able to meet their needs. If you are sick, it will affect all of your interactions with your family, from your ability to meet their basic needs for nutrition and safety, to your ability to make good parenting decisions and run around with them. Add to that the fact that you are the most influential health role model for your children, and you have a very good reason to focus time and attention on your health.

Body and Soul

If you are spiritual or religious, and believe in the presence of a soul (or similar term, such as spirit, force or source), the health of your body is very closely related to the health of your soul. Your body provides an amazing home for your soul, and it is connected and communicating with your soul continuously. A healthy body will nourish your soul and allow its true brilliance and energy to shine and share its gifts with the world.

A positive model for health

The World Health Organization has defined health as "a state of complete physical, mental and social well-being and not merely the absence of disease or infirmity", since 1947. This positive model of health recognizes the health as being holistic and connected to other aspects of wellbeing. Sadly, much medical practice follows a model of treating disease and infirmity, and neglects the wider goal of improving all aspects of wellbeing.

If you adopt a positive model of health, it is possible to:

- Prevent illness
- Increase the number of years in good health
- Extend lifespan
- Improve mental and physical health
- Improve outcomes when illness strikes
- Reduce stress and other risk factors
- Improve life satisfaction
- Reduce health care expenditure and
- Improve the health and wellbeing of your loved ones.

Your health, your responsibility

Most members of the medical profession have a noble aim to respect human life and consider the health of their patients, to the best of their ability. However, when I was a doctor, I became aware that my profession rarely made people better; instead, we facilitated the body making itself better.

When you are sick, it is important to avoid handing over total responsibility for your health, to others. For most people, with most diseases, improving lifestyle factors such as diet and exercise will improve their outcome. Taking care of yourself is not a guarantee for good health, but you will certainly be stacking the odds in your favor. There are of course tragic accidents or devastating illnesses where there is little you can do to change your outcome, but these are rare.

Poor health is a continuum: During your life the majority of cells, organs or systems of your body are functioning normally: Maintaining health and equilibrium. Illness is caused by abnormal functioning of some cells, organs or systems. When you are in poor health, it is important to keep focused on the fact that your body is working hard to restore balance and health. You can either help or hinder it.

When you are in poor health, it is not the time to feel sorry for yourself and engage in bad habits. When you are sick, your body deserves to be nurtured, nourished, hydrated and rested: Not filled with foods, poisons or thoughts that slow the body's ability to heal.

The Balance of Health Model

The Balance of Health Model is a simplistic, yet powerful approach to helping your body achieve balance and health. Think of your health as being like a bank account: You have assets and liabilities.

The Balance of Health

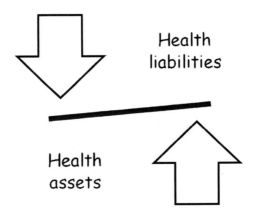

Health liabilities

Health assets

To improve your health, look for opportunities to increase health assets and decrease health liabilities.

Health assets include:
1. Healthy diet
2. Hydration
3. Positive thinking (Chapter 7)
4. Self-regulation (Chapter 4)
5. Exercise
6. Sleep

7. Healthy habits (Chapter 8)
8. Positive relationships (Chapter 8)
9. Genetics
10. Hygiene
11. New learning

Health liabilities include:

1. Dehydration
2. Unhealthy diet
3. Inactivity
4. Engaging in unhealthy habits such as smoking, excessive alcohol intake or drug taking
5. Avoiding medical care for medical problems
6. Contact with poisons
7. Contact with infections
8. Physical harm
9. Emotional harm, including stress (Chapter 7)
10. Extremes of weight
11. Genetics

Exercise 6.1 Your Healthy Intuition

Print the exercise from the workbook or answer questions in your journal.

- What does good health mean to you?
- What areas of your health would you like to improve?
- Would you be willing to accept optimal health, energy, vitality and strength?
- How would your life be different if you had optimal health, energy, vitality and strength?
- When you feel ill, stressed, in pain or tired, how do you know? What messages does your body send you?
- How does your body feel when you do something that you know is good for it (like eating a healthy meal or exercising?)

- How does your body feel when you do something that you know is bad for it (like eating an unhealthy meal, getting drunk or spending the day watching TV)?
- What has your amazing body allowed you to accomplish, in your life?
- What has poor health prevented you from accomplishing, in your life so far?

What does your intuition tell you about:

- Things that harm you?
- Things that are good for you?
- Food you should eat?
- Food you should not eat?
- The drinks you should drink?
- The drinks you should not drink?
- The exercise you should take?
- The sleep and rest you should have?
- How your habits help or hinder you?
- How your relationships affect your health?
- How your health affects your overall wellbeing?
- The help and health advice you should seek out?
- What are your top three health assets? See list above.
- What are your top three health liabilities?

The rest of the chapter is devoted to further discussion on physical health assets and liabilities.

Food and Eating

Here's a question you may not have considered: Why do you eat? There are several possible reasons:

- Nutrition
- Hunger
- Thirst

- Taste
- Time to eat: Sometimes people eat for no other reason other than it's time, this is most common for breakfast. Children mainly eat when adults tell them.
- Impulsivity
- Entertainment
- Pleasure: We see food, smell it or even think of it and expect to feel pleasure when we eat it.
- Craving
- Addiction
- Social interaction
- To change the way we feel, physically
- To change the way we look
- To change the way we feel, emotionally: Sometimes we eat to relieve boredom, sadness, anger or ease stress
- To exert power over others: Other people may be able to control some aspects of your life, but they can't control the food you put in your mouth.

Nutrition

If you want to have a healthy body it is vital to consider the nutritional value of the food you eat.

Food fuels our body. You can chose to put high quality fuel into your body or poor quality fuel, and this choice will affect its performance. Sure we can live on a diet of junk food, and we might live many years. But over time this food will cause cumulative damage to the body. Food contains nutrients, the materials necessary to support life.

Food has nutritional and non-nutritional components:

- Macronutrients (we need large amounts): carbohydrates, proteins, fats and water.
- Micronutrients (we need small amounts): vitamins and minerals.
- Non-nutrients: the parts of the food we don't need. Some of these are not absorbed into our blood stream (such as fiber) but still benefit our

body. Others are absorbed into our body, have no nutritional value and cause damage to our cells; many of these are found in highly processed foods. These damaging substances include:

- Antibiotics given to food-producing animals
- Many factory-made additives such as aspartame, artificial colors and sweeteners and MSG have no nutritional value and can be damaging to health.

Simple Food Rules

There are so many conflicting sources of information on what we should eat. Here's a simple guide that a ten year old could follow:

- Eat mostly fresh food, raw or cooked. Fresh foods include: Fruit, vegetables, plant based proteins like lentils or chickpeas, grains, seeds or nuts. Tony Robbins teaches in many of his courses to aim for at least 70% of the food on your plate being naturally rich in water. Different foods contain different nutrients, so aim for variety.
- Limit processed food. I recommend avoiding any food with more than ten ingredients and food containing ingredients that sound like they were made in a lab (see dirty dozen above).
- Limit alcohol and coffee. In small amounts may be mildly beneficial but in excess are harmful.
- Avoid any food that makes you feel unwell or tired. Listen to your body: It's trying to tell you what not to eat.
- Choose supplements wisely. For fit, healthy people, eating a healthy balanced diet is best. Doing so, however, can be challenging, expensive and time consuming. For healthy people my top three recommendations are: High-quality fish oil, vitamin D and a pro-biotic. The benefits of vitamin supplements are controversial; with some research showing poor "bio-availability" (your body doesn't digest or process well). Consider a "whole food nutrition" supplement instead. If you have a specific health problem or are in a specific life stage such as pregnancy, ask your doctor if there are other supplements

you could take. Always read the warning list on any supplement and do not take them if you are unsure.

- Watch your protein. We only need about 10 percent of our intake to be protein. Limit red meat consumption to twice a week, maximum. Eat fish up to twice a week.

- Eat smaller portions, more often, more slowly and with more focus. Your body is not designed for "all you can eat buffets" and you are not a komodo dragon, who can swallow a foal whole, hooves and all! Eating three main meals a day, with healthy snacks in between, suits most people. Eating slowly and chewing food well, can prevent overeating and aid digestion.

- Control your environment. Plan healthy meals and snacks ahead of time and shop accordingly. You may have good intentions, but if your cupboards are full of unhealthy food, you may self sabotage.

- Encourage the people around you to eat healthily: It will make you feel more comfortable, and you will be giving them all the wonderful benefits of a good diet. My youngest son recently said to me in the grocery store "if you loved me, you'd let me have a bottle of "G." "G" is a "sports" drink in the USA. I replied "because I love you I am not going to let you have "G."It contains harmful food colorings and high fructose corn syrup." Pester power can be hard to resist, so set up rules in advance.

Eat the right diet for you, and you will feel energetic, your skin will look good, and you will get ill less often. You will also recover more quickly, when you do get ill. You will be more productive as well, and you may have better relationships. Just by eating the right foods in the right amounts, you can reduce your risk of chronic illness such as cancer, dementia and health disease and ultimately increase your lifespan.

Eat the wrong diet and you will feel tired and unmotivated. Your skin will look unhealthy; you will get ill more often and for longer. You will underperform and may even find yourself being irritable with your loved ones. Finally, eating poorly will probably increase your chances of chronic illness and premature death.

Changing what you eat

Begin with education. Find a reputable source of information on nutrition and decide what foods you are going to eat (for more information visit the website at www.beyondsoccermom/health). The next step is to become consciously aware of what you are eating and why.

Exercise 6.1 Mindful eating

Step 1. Think about why you eat.

Review the list below and consider the frequency with which you eat for each reason (often, sometimes, never). Sometimes we eat to meet more than one need at a time. If the frequency is sometimes or often, think of an alternative behavior that would better meet this need. Examples: If you think you are thirsty, drink a large glass of water. If you are bored, do something interesting or active. If you want to exert power over others, consider talking to them instead.

Reasons for eating:

- Nutrition
- Hunger
- Thirst
- Taste
- Time to eat
- Impulsivity (I just want to)
- Entertainment
- Pleasure
- Craving
- Addiction
- Social interaction
- To change the way I feel physically
- To change the way I feel emotionally e.g. if you are bored, sad, angry or stressed
- To change the way I look
- To exert power over others
- Other…

Step 2. Print or copy the list of needs and put them in places where you store food or keep the list with you. Before you start eating, determine which need is driving you to eat. Make a conscious decision: Eat or do something else.

Step 3. When you eat, try to eat slowly and mindfully. Think about how the food looks, its texture, smell and taste, where the food comes from and its nutritional value.

The exercise above has helped many people draw conscious attention to what they are eating and allowed them to take control of their eating. There are times when it is entirely appropriate to eat for entertainment, social interaction and to change the way we feel physically or look (within sensible limits). If you are eating because of an addiction like coffee or sugar, then you may need to consider taking additional action to overcome your addiction. Chapter 7 has a section on habits. If you have an addiction, a significant problem with emotional eating, suffer from extremes of weight or are eating to exert power over others, please consider getting professional help.

Tracking what you eat

There is a general consensus that one of the best ways to manage what you eat, is to track what you eat. This process makes you consciously aware of your intake of food and reduces impulse eating and eating too much over the day. There are many measures of the quality of food of which calories, glycaemic index and Nu-Val are but three. There are many different versions of food journals (including apps); they vary in complexity and in my opinion, quality.

If you are looking for a very simple way to track what you and your family eat, try Exercise 6.2. It was designed for my boys when they were under seven. It relies on your evaluation of what is healthy. If you want your children to use it, first talk to them about healthy eating and why it is important. Consider completing for a few days and maybe even competing against each other.

Exercise 6.2 Nutrition Journal

Complete the exercise from the workbook or create a table, with 3 columns: 1= food or drink item, 2 = nutrition score, 3 = running total. For the entire day, write down everything you eat and drink.

Nutrition score examples:

5 = raw vegetables or fruit, unprocessed plant based protein

4 = cooked vegetables or fruit, glass of filtered water (up to 6 per day), drinks like green or fruit tea

3 = unprocessed/ homemade meat or fish, eggs

2 = processed healthy food, such as yoghurt, homemade simple baked goods, good quality granola bar, fruit drink (only the first glass each day) BUT not if they contain harmful substances like MSG, aspartamine, artificial food coloring, hydrogenated fat

1 = some processed food such as cereal, bread, cakes, cookies etc BUT not if they contain harmful substances like MSG, aspartamine, artificial food coloring or hydrogenated fat

0 = less healthy processed food

-1 = anything containing harmful substances like MSG, aspartamine, artificial food coloring, hydrogenated fat

-2 = anything containing multiple harmful substances for example some diet sodas and candy.

Hydration

Every cell in your body needs water. Water has many functions: It flushes out toxins, forms a key constituent of all cells, carries nutrients to cells and creates a moist environment for ear, nose and throat tissues. About 60 percent (range 50-75) of your body's weight is water. The Institute of Medicine recommends that men consume the equivalent of about 125 ounces (8 pints) of water daily and that women consume about 91 ounces (5.5 pints), including intake from all foods and beverages.

Most of us don't need to over-think this. Certain groups need to be more "purposeful" about their drinking, such as people who live in a hot environment, people who are exercising vigorously for long periods, or individuals who have specific illnesses, such as kidney disease and diabetes.

Intake also depends on age (children need more) and gender (women need less than men, unless pregnant).

The body is constantly losing water in breath, perspiration, urine and feces. For your body to function properly, you must replenish its water supply by consuming water-rich food and drink. The water in food accounts for about 20 percent of the average person's total daily water intake. Most foods contain some water; even a bagel contains about 33 percent water. Some foods obviously contain more water, such as an apple (84 percent) and broccoli (91 percent). These naturally water-rich foods often have the added benefit of being nutrient rich.

When engaging in moderate exercise, you should be aiming to take a drink every 20 minutes. Listen to your body: If you are thirsty, you have needed to drink for a while.

Without a doubt the best drink for hydration is clean, fresh water. Some foods and drinks are dehydrating, such as salty foods, alcoholic beverages, caffeinated, highly processed or sugary food or drink.

The quality of water is also important. Water should be free from organisms, poisons and toxins. Avoid, when possible, drinking water from bottles which contain BPA (a chemical found in some plastics, which the FDA confirms is harmful to health at high levels).

Signs of dehydration include: Thirst, urine looking dark like apple juice, decreased urine output, dry, sticky mouth, lack of energy, dry skin, headache, constipation, dizziness and confusion. Mild dehydration is implicated in many cases of recurrent headache, attention difficulties and constipation in both adults and children.

Increasing water intake may also be useful in the battle against excess weight by lowering calorie intake, increasing metabolism and reducing hunger. If you struggle with overeating, try for one week, drinking a glass of water every time you feel hungry and then wait for five minutes. If you are still hungry, then eat.

Exercise

If you could buy a product that would make you better looking and more intelligent, as well as more healthy, happy, energetic and fun, would you buy it?

Of course you would. Well, it's not a product you need, its exercise. The only cost is your time.

Most of us know that exercise is good, so why is it that so many of us struggle to do it regularly? Here are some of the most commonly encountered reasons for not exercising:

- I don't have time
- I have too much to do
- I'm tired
- I'm not in the habit
- I can't be bothered
- I'm not motivated
- It's overwhelming
- I've got no one to go with
- I'm too unfit or I am ill
- I can't afford a gym membership
- I tried it but I didn't see a difference
- I don't like exercising
- It's boring
- It hurts
- I'm embarrassed
- I don't know what to do
- I put on weight when I exercise

The next exercise will help you address any mindset barriers to exercising.

Exercise 6.3 Change your mind about exercise. Part 1
Think about exercising.

Notice any negative or crooked thinking you have about exercise.

Write them down.

Are you 100 percent sure that these thoughts are true?

There is a HUGE amount of scientific evidence that exercise is good for you. Exercise is good for you for many different reasons, but especially because it:

- Improves blood flow to your brain and your whole body.
- Improves your brain capacity. According to Daniel Amen's research, exercise encourages growth of new brain cells, enhances cognitive ability and makes you more productive.
- Burns calories. Whether you do a 30 minute bike ride, go on a long walk or have a day where you are very active in the house or garden, it all helps.
- Reduces the risk of illness. Frequent exercisers have a decreased risk of most illnesses including dementia, heart disease, stroke, cancer and osteoporosis.
- Improves the outcome of illness. Exercise reduces symptoms caused by many health issues, including ADHD, Alzheimer's and diabetes, among others.
- Improves mood. Exercise alleviates depression, worry and anxiety by producing mood-enhancing neurochemicals and improving blood flow to the brain.
- Boosts energy.
- Makes you look better. Exercise is good for your skin. It makes you look younger and more attractive by increasing circulation, increasing collagen production, reducing stress hormones (which have a negative effect on skin) and reducing inflammation.
- Promotes better sleep.
- Improves sex life: people who exercise regularly have higher libido and more energy during sex.
- Can be fun. If you find an exercise that you find fun, you will have a double benefit. The first time I went to a Zumba class everyone laughed all the way through. You might want to try combining exercise on a machine with another activity you enjoy such as watching TV, listening to music or reading a book.
- Improves strength, co-ordination, agility, speed and flexibility. All of this helps you to keep up with your kids and catch them when they fall.

Exercise 6.3 Change your mind, about exercise. Part 2

Write out the list below or read the following out loud:

- Exercise is an investment in my future health.
- Exercise improves my health.
- Exercise increases my energy.
- Exercise improves my metabolism.
- Exercise improves the health of every cell in my body.
- Exercise makes happy chemicals for my brain.
- Exercise can make me more intelligent and successful.
- Exercise makes my brain work better.
- Exercise improves the health of my skin.
- Exercise makes me strong.
- Exercise can be fun.
- Exercise is about movement.
- I can make time to exercise.

Did you have trouble with saying any of these statements?

Go back to your negative thoughts list and see if you can find a statement, from the list, that would counteract your negative one.

Add your own positive statement if you can think of one.

When you notice yourself having a negative thought about exercise, say it out loud and challenge it.

If you are struggling to exercise, print the list and put it on your bathroom mirror, repeat out loud daily for 21 days.

Types of exercise

One of the problems with exercising is that there are so many options and opinions, it can be overwhelming. The key is to find an exercise program that is right for you: This means exercise that you enjoy, that doesn't feel like a chore and that progressively increases your fitness.

You should try to include in your weekly exercise:

1. Aerobic exercise
2. Muscle strengthening
3. Core exercises
4. Co-ordination exercises

Warning

Here's the mandatory warning that comes with exercise: All exercises can be dangerous. Before starting any new exercise consider consulting your doctor, especially if you have a chronic health problem, recurring injury or are pregnant or nursing. If you experience pain, breathlessness or dizziness while exercising, stop immediately and consider consulting your doctor if symptoms are significant or severe.

How to improve your exercise regime

- Complete exercise 3.1 "Personal Development Plan" (Chapter 3) for exercise. Be clear about your motivation. Set goals realistically. For exercise, set a goal that relates to frequency of exercise. Remember exercise will improve your health, but it is not guaranteed to make you lose weight.
- Be really creative and flexible. Exercise is about getting moving and there are many, many alternatives: Gardening, on-line exercise videos, walking, running up and down stairs, riding a horse, doing push-ups, Pilates, skipping, apps on your phone, yoga, martial arts, dancing, running, swimming, kicking a soccer ball, using gym equipment, fitness video games, riding a bike, playing basketball, skiing, lifting dumb-bells in your bedroom and so on. Try and find something you enjoy, love, or at least can tolerate.
- Start small. Begin with baby steps and build up intensity and time.
- Stop if you experience pain. Any sharp or sudden onset pain is your body telling you to stop. Some aching when you begin a new exercise is normal, listen to your body.
- Get help. Get support from your kids, your partner, friends, an accountability partner, support group, forum or a coach.
- Check with your doctor. If you are carrying excess weight, have an injury, chronic illness or are pregnant before starting a new exercise routine, see the doctor first.
- Optimize your nutrition if you are exercising more.

- Persevere. Over time, it gets easier. Make a plan and stick to it. At first you may not enjoy it, but over time working out not only becomes tolerable but actually begins to feel necessary.
- Make it a habit. The more often you exercise, the more chance there is of it becoming a habit. Once an activity becomes a habit, it becomes almost effortless. If you really want exercise to become a habit, commit to doing something every day, for at least a month (see chapter 7, section on habits)
- Remember something is better than nothing. If you have a very busy day and can only manage five minutes, it is better than nothing. Look for opportunities to increase your activity doing what you have to do, like parking at the far end of the parking-lot or taking the stairs.
- Stop making excuses. It's your body and your health; no one else is going to do it. Remember: Exercise a great investment in your health.
- Mix it up. If you get bored easily, have different activities planned every week.
- Multitask. If you really don't enjoy exercise, add in a pleasurable activity, such as watching TV on the treadmill, listening to music while you run, or chatting to a friend while lifting weights.
- Tap into your friends. Make a conscious effort to spend time with people who enjoy exercise, and allow them to inspire, motivate and encourage you.
- Track your exercise. Make use of the wealth of tools available to track your exercise from simple pedometers to apps on your phone. Like with food tracking helps you consciously process how much exercise you are doing. One client told me "I move more now because I now know how little I move naturally during a typical day. Knowledge is power."

Phew now that we've addressed exercise let's think about sleep!

Sleep

Good sleep improves health, wellbeing and performance. It is essential to your body's ability to repair and process. Poor sleep can make you ill, unhappy and underperform in everything you do.

Sleep facts:

- Approximately one in five adults suffers from a sleep problem. Sleep problems have serious consequences to the health of individuals and the population. As a result, poor sleep causes significant health care and productivity costs.
- The average adult needs seven to eight hours of good quality sleep.
- Getting enough good quality sleep can help you:
  ◊ Reach and maintain a stable weight
  ◊ Have better looking skin
  ◊ Improve focus, performance and memory
  ◊ Regulate your mood
  ◊ Reduce your risk of chronic diseases such as dementia, stroke and diabetes

Sleep problems

For moms these include:

- Your little darling waking you during the night
- Medications and caffeine
- Stress, worry, anxiety and depression
- Pregnancy, PMS, perimenopause and menopause (don't you love being a woman!)
- Sharing a bed or room with a snorer
- Health problems
- Poor bedtime routine or uncomfortable bed

Sleep deprivation

Sleep deprivation is getting less sleep than you need. Sleep deprivation is a major cause of accidents and can cause or worsen:

- Overeating carbohydrates and gaining weight,
- Unhealthy skin,
- Poor focus and willpower,
- Depression and anxiety in all ages groups,

- Poor sports performance,
- Changeable mood,
- Bad habits, such as coffee, smoking, lack of exercise and illegal drugs,
- Diabetes. Sleeplessness increases insulin resistance and glucose intolerance,
- Worsening of symptoms of illness,
- Traffic accidents.

Sleep apnea

Sleep apnea is a serious medical condition in which breathing stops, intermittently, for short periods, during sleep. If sleep apnea is suspected, medical advice must be sought as it is associated high blood pressure, heart disease, stroke, Alzheimer's, daytime fatigue, attention and memory problems, morning headaches and emotional problems.

Sleep Plan

Just like any other change, if you want better sleep you need a plan:

- Establish consistent sleep habits: Try and go to bed at the same time every night and get up at the same time every morning. Make sure your bed is comfortable, your room is warm, and your sleep space is as dark as you can tolerate.
- Plan for daily down time: During the day plan some relaxation time to prevent you from getting overwhelmed or stressed.
- Engage in calming activities at night. Find something relaxing to do before bed, like reading, meditating, taking a bath, or listening to music or a relaxation recording. Avoid television if it prevents you from sleeping.
- Use background noise. Consider a white noise machine or fan, to distract your mind from negative thoughts or environmental noise.
- Avoid day-time naps. If you need to rest during the day, try to avoid going to sleep by doing something relaxing. Clearly, there are exceptions like when you are ill, your child is having a disturbed night or you are nursing.

- Turn off electronics in the bedroom.
- Pay attention to what you eat and drink. If you notice a pattern of food or drink that helps or hinders good sleep, take action.
- Exercise: Make sure you have exercised in the day. Exercise tires you out and increases levels of hormones and neurochemicals that help you sleep.
- Address night-time waking. You naturally enter a state of light sleep several times each night. During this time, you are more likely to wake up if you are worried, in pain or are cold or if there is external noise. If you wake during the night, try one of these:
  ◊ Think about your favorite movie or book. Try and retell the story from the beginning to yourself in as much detail as you can.
  ◊ Listen to a relaxation recording
  ◊ Think about a favorite place or event. Recall it in as much detail as you can.
- If you are still having trouble sleeping after consistently trying this plan for one week, consider trying a natural supplement such as melatonin or 5-HTP but please read the label and/or check with a doctor.
- See a doctor if:
  ◊ You think you may have sleep apnea
  ◊ You have serious or long-standing sleep deprivation
  ◊ You have recurrent early morning wakening
  ◊ You think medications are interfering with sleep.

Please make sure they try non-addictive treatments first.

Genetics

Our genes are a set of instructions that determine what we are like: From our eye color to the shape of our nose. At the cellular level, genes determine what the cell becomes, how long it survives, and how it behaves in its environment. Genes determine the risk of certain diseases or disorders. The presence of some genes makes it certain that that individual will have a disease, such as cystic fibrosis or Down's syndrome, although this may change in the near future, with advances in genetic engineering. Other genes make us more or less susceptible to problems, like high cholesterol or autism. It remains to be seen whether lifestyle and environmental factors can change DNA. There is, however, increasing evidence that these factors can affect the expression of some genes and therefore, susceptibility to disease. One study showed that lifestyle changes altered the gene expression of over 500 genes, which in turn improved health. Lifestyle can also affect the longevity of our cells and therefore, our bodies.

Avoid poisons and physical harm

When it's worded like this it seems like a no-brainer; after all, who would knowingly expose themselves to poisons or physical harm?

Unfortunately, harmful substances are all around us, some are even socially acceptable. Culprits include cigarettes, excessive alcohol, illegal drugs, some prescriptions drugs, contaminants in water and chemicals used in food. Many harmful substances in our environment are hidden, and some affect only some individuals. For example: If you know you are allergic to peanuts, for you peanuts are a poison. Likewise, if you are a diabetic, a sugared donut is effectively a poison to you.

We can't completely avoid the risk of physical harm, but we can reduce it, just like we make sure there are no toys on the stairs and that we drive safely.

When it comes to our children, we have to weigh up the risks and advantages of certain activities. Children need to be active in order to thrive, but some activities are more inherently dangerous than others, like playing football or riding a bike on busy roads.

If you knowingly expose yourself or your children to something which you know is harmful, you make a choice. Start with educating yourself about risks and then make an informed decision, on how to raise your children.

Sensible hygiene

Now I don't want to scare you, but there are infectious agents everywhere. Some are potentially harmful; some are insignificant, and others are even helpful. Everyday hygiene routines such as washing your hands, with soap, after using the toilet, before a meal or preparing food, using a handkerchief when sneezing, brushing your teeth twice a day and washing fresh food before eating, should protect healthy people from most infections. Common infections like colds and tummy bugs are hard to prevent but healthy people should recover quickly from these.

Seeking appropriate medical care

There are times when you might need medical care, for example, when we are acutely ill (sudden onset, short duration), chronically ill (persistent or recurrent) or pregnant. For minor problems or complaints, however, try simple measures first. For example, if you have a mild headache, try resting, increasing fluid intake and taking a simple painkiller. A good healthcare professional should consider both medical and lifestyle causes and treatments for your health problem. Keeping an accurate record of your medical history will help any healthcare professional provide better care.

When it comes to the health of children, err on the side of caution and trust your intuition. If you feel that there is something "not right" with your child, seek advice.

Watching your weight

Extremes of weight are harmful to your health. I have struggled with my weight for over 20 years and know how difficult it can be to reach and sustain a healthy weight.

Most diets work for some people, for some time, but often weight creeps back on. I believe that part of the problem, with people struggling to maintain a healthy weight is fad diets, which are unsustainable or overcomplicated, and the ever changing advice from "experts". The weight loss industry in the US alone is worth over $60 billion a year and there are thousands of books on losing weight and healthy eating.

The NIH puts weight gain simply: "Overweight and obesity happen over time when you take in more calories than you use."

The secret to optimizing weight

There's a secret that the weight loss industry would rather you didn't know. This secret is rather simple.

- Optimize nutrition: Nutrition depends on the food we ingest (see earlier in this chapter) and the health of our digestive and other systems that help nutrients get to our cells.
- Optimize energy use: Energy use is affected by metabolism in our cells and by the amount of energy we expend by moving (see exercise section above) and our bodily processes, which burn fuel.
- Overcome barriers to change: Here is where the challenge lies for many people!

The secret to optimizing weight

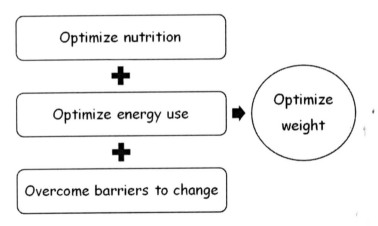

Overcoming barriers to optimizing weight

- Your mind: Your conscious mind may desire you to be an optimal weight, but unconscious processes may sabotage you. These include emotional eating, crooked thinking about food, self image and exercise. More on this in chapter 7.
- Your diet: Lack of knowledge about nutritious food is very common. When you were at school, you may have received little or no education, on nutrition. If you were lucky, your parents may have taught you about nutrition and how to cook. Over the last 100 years the nutritional quality of readily available food, has changed dramatically. It is now easier and cheaper to access highly-processed cookies than locally-produced fruit and vegetables.

- Your lifestyle: Your lifestyle is very different from that of your great-grandmother, who probably led a physically active lifestyle: Cleaning, doing laundry by hand (including diapers), walking to the grocery store and making meals with basic equipment. Labor-saving devices have lead to the need for many women to actively seek out activities to get moving.

- Your environment: We are all affected by a modern-day environment that can counteract our best efforts to stay fit. Many of us lack access to safe walking areas and nutritious foods, even as we have easy access to television and to calorie-rich food. What's more, a powerful food industry's has many ingenious ways of steering us towards cheap, long-lasting, processed food – and away from healthy, nutrient-rich whole foods.

- Your genes and family history: Rarely there can be a strong genetic risk for being overweight. For most people, however, genetics are not that significant. Lifestyle changes can change the expression of genes that affect weight. Don't see yourself as a victim of genetics.

- Your current health: Many health problems can affect your ability to either optimize nutrition or optimize energy use. These include physical disability or injury, hormonal imbalance, underactive thyroid, diabetes and polycystic ovarian syndrome. However, people with these conditions can still significantly improve their health (and reduce symptoms) by adopting a more nutritious diet and increasing exercise. Medical treatment of these conditions will also help optimize weight.

- Your medicines: Some medicines can affect nutrition and energy expenditure or cause fluid retention. If you are concerned that you are taking such medicines, discuss options with your doctor.

- Smoking: Stopping smoking can cause an often temporary increase in weight. However, the health benefits of quitting far outweigh the risk of gaining a few pounds.

- Age: Unfortunately, as you get older you tend to lose muscle and this in turn slows the rate at which your body burns calories. Menopause adds to the effect by altering metabolism. So if you are finding you are piling on the pounds as you age, it is even more important to focus on your nutrition and activities which strengthen muscles.

- Pregnancy and breastfeeding: Weight gain in pregnancy and breastfeeding is normal, within limits. You'll need to increase your calorie intake, but this should not be at the cost of nutrition. Eating a nutritious diet in pregnancy will give your baby an excellent head start, for their future health and brain development. Being pregnant and having a young baby can make it difficult to find the time to exercise, but it's important to get at least some gentle, regular exercise. Be kind to yourself but don't use this period of your life as an excuse to neglect your health. Get advice from your doctor and or a reputable health site like WebMD on appropriate nutrition and exercise during this stage of your life.
- Lack of Sleep: Sleep deprivation affects eating habits (crave calories and carbohydrates) and affects the hunger and satiation (full) hormones, along with insulin the hormone that controls blood sugar.

For more information on managing weight see www.beyondsoccermom/resources.

Risks of being carrying excess weight

Most people who carry extra weight are well aware that excess weights increases health risk. Chances are even if you have been living under a rock, you are probably aware of at least some risks of being overweight. My reasons for sharing the lengthy list below are not to scare you, but to make you consciously aware. When you have read the list, acknowledge that there are many good reasons to focus on your health and take action, but do not dwell on the list.

Carrying excess weight increases your risk of:

- Coronary heart disease
- High blood pressure
- Stroke
- Type 2 diabetes
- Abnormal blood fats
- Metabolic syndrome (a group of risk factors that raises your risk for heart disease and other health problems, such as diabetes and stroke)
- Cancer (including colon, breast, endometrial, and gallbladder cancers)

- Osteoarthritis and osteoporosis
- Sleep apnea
- Reproductive problems (menstrual issues and infertility in women)
- Gallstones
- Dementia
- Feeling uncomfortable
- Social anxiety
- Poor self-esteem
- Gym phobia

Exercise 6.4 Optimizing Weight Plan

Complete exercise 3.2 "Personal Development Plan" for your weight problem or see the Optimizing Weight Plan in the workbook.

Health and your family

At the same time as you are taking steps to ensure you are in good health, I am sure you will be taking steps to ensure that your children and other family members are, too.

The healthy habits you teach your child will last them a lifetime and give them an excellent start in life. Conversely, unhealthy habits and poor lifestyle choices in childhood may affect the health of your child. Some of the negative effects may be invisible right now, but long term they will cause harm and eventually illness.

Pester power can a very challenging barrier to a healthy lifestyle in children. So if you want your child to change their lifestyle, start by educating them. Schools may provide some useful health information for children, but the quality is very variable. Knowing how your child reacts to change will help you decide whether to make changes rapidly or gradually. For example, some children may respond well to you suddenly making them eat more vegetables with dinner; for others, you may have to be cunning and blend vegetables into other foods.

Keep in mind that you are the boss and it is your role to keep your child safe and thriving. Set clear boundaries for your child and be consistent. For example if you change the bedtime routine, be explicit with your child about the new rules and your reasons for them. Then consistently enforce the new rules.

As your family's health improves you may notice that relationships flourish, and you may experience a greater abundance of success and fun! Worth a try, don't you think?

Exercise 6.5 Health Mantra

Stand and repeat out loud:

- My body is amazing.
- My body is striving to keep me healthy.
- I am working with my body to be healthy.
- I love to exercise and feel energetic.
- I love to eat healthy, nutritious food.
- I deserve restful sleep.
- Being healthy will help me become happy and successful.
- Health is my greatest wealth.

Chapter 6 Summary

Your health, and that of each family member, is precious.

Your body is constantly working hard to maintain health and balance.

You have a choice whether to help or hinder your body.

The health of your body affects wellbeing, performance and success in all areas of your life.

Health is a balancing act. If you want better health, look for ways to increase your health assets and decrease your health liabilities.

Take responsibility for your health.

Take responsibility for the health of your children, and be a good role model. This will give your kids a great head start in developing healthy habits, preventing chronic illness and optimizing brain development.

Chapter 7

HEALTHY MIND

The human brain and mind are truly remarkable, complex yet capable of constant change and evolution. The human brain and mind can do amazing things: Thinking, feeling, perceiving, communicating, inventing, creating, loving, learning, imagining, dreaming, calculating and so on. It is the extraordinary complexity of the brain and mind that make us unique individuals.

Amazing facts about your brain and mind
- The average adult brain weighs 3lbs.
- The brain is about 70 percent water.
- The brain contains 1.1 trillion cells, of which 100 billion are nerve cells.
- The nervous system and brain transmits signals by a combination of electrical and chemical signals. The brain generates between 10-23 watts of power, enough to power a light bulb.
- The brain is 2 percent of the body's weight but uses 20-25 percent of the body's oxygen and glucose.

- When we think or move, there is activity in complex temporary and permanent groups of nerve cells.
- The brain is constantly communicating with the rest of your body via the circulatory, nervous, and hormonal systems.
- New neural pathways are being formed continually until the day we die. This is called Neuroplasticity and is the foundation of how we can learn new things and change our behavior.
- The brain is involved with almost everything you do.
- If your brain is working well, you will significantly increase the chances of your mind working well and being happy, healthy and successful.
- Your brain can seem tough, but you must treat it with respect, for it is delicate and easily damaged.
- Anything that is good for your brain is likely to be good for your body, your looks, your mind, your relationships and your performance.
- Your brain and mind are constantly working; although some parts can be in a resting state, others continue working.

Neuroscience research has lead to remarkable insights into how our brain and mind work. The most accessible of this is to be found in the many books by Dr. Daniel Amen. His research using SPECT scans (scans showing real-time brain function) provide powerful insight into what is good for our brain and what is not.

Your mind

- As touched on in Chapter 4, the mind is the flow of chemical and electrical signals within the brain. These signals relate to information to and from sources external to our body (including interactions with other people) and internal within our body and the brain itself. The function of our mind affects our thoughts, feelings, memories, attitudes, beliefs, dreams, ideas and actions.

Your mind is constantly working and developing. Development begins before birth and continues throughout our life. It is affected by events in your life, including, traumas both physical and emotional, conflicts, the environment, society, education, relationships, upbringing and the health of your brain.

We each have a unique mind, capable of many things from the mundane, like writing a shopping list, to the amazing, like composing a symphony or running a Fortune 500 company. There are people whose minds who can perform superhuman tasks (savants), such as Daniel Tammet, who learned Icelandic in a week and memorized pi to 22,514 decimal places, or Stephen Wiltshire who can draw an accurate and detailed city landscape after seeing it only once.

There are many theories about the mind, but I'm sure most of us have heard of Freud, the father of psychology. Simply put, he concluded that the mind has three main parts: The conscious mind (the part you are aware of), the preconscious (the part that is easily brought to awareness) and the subconscious (the part hidden away and repressed). Think of your subconscious mind as being like that box hidden in your attic or basement, full of stuff that you had forgotten you had. When you look closely you realize that your subconscious mind is full of a lot of hidden gems and useless junk!

The human mind is also like an iceberg: The conscious mind above the water (about 10%), the subconscious and preconscious below the water (about 90%). Much of the time your conscious mind is running the show, but it is constantly influenced and fed by the subconscious mind.

In the rest of this chapter, we will consider four aspects of the health of the mind:

- Thinking
- Stress
- Habits
- Confidence

The study of the mind is a vast field, so I have picked these four aspects that often prevent moms from achieving their goals. Each will be discussed, along with exercises to help you improve that aspect of mind health. If you have a significant problem with the health of your mind, please seek professional advice.

Thinking

Your thoughts change the way you perceive the world, the way you behave and the way you interact. Your thoughts even change the electrical and chemical signals in your brain and the rhythm of your heart. It is empowering to know that you can change your thoughts in an instant. Have you ever felt sad or angry, and then something funny happens, and you can't help but laugh and feel happy, even if it's just for a moment? This change happens because your thoughts have changed in an instant. You can learn to control your thoughts if you want to.

Neuroscience has shown that positive thinking enhances brain function, while negative thinking worsens brain function, especially in the parts of the brain concerned with balance, co-ordination, processing, emotional regulation and social skills. Yes, you read correctly: Negative thinking can make you clumsy and stupid.

SO here's a question for you: "What kind of thinker are you?"

- A "glass half empty" (pessimist),
- A "glass half full" (optimist),
- A "half of a glass" (realist) or
- A "what does the glass mean anyway" (philosopher)?

Crooked thinking

The human mind is like a computer in that it can store, process and retrieve large amounts of information. But, there is one major problem with the human mind, however: Some of the information stored in the mind is not correct, and this incorrect information can lead to inaccurate or negative thinking.

Some of the information stored in your mind:

- Was never true: You dreamed it, imagined it or misinterpreted it.
- Was true once, but is no longer true.
- Was stored with a false association.

Sometimes we believe something that we dream or imagine; dreams can be very vivid and seem very real. Sometimes we believe information which, it later turns out, we have misheard or misinterpreted. I worked with a girl who heard her step-dad and mother discussing whether they should adopt her. She thought they wanted to give her to another family and was upset for weeks, only to find out they meant that her step-dad would legally become her guardian.

Many people go through life believing something that was once but is no longer, true. Like a girl who fails one important test and goes on to believe she is a failure for the rest of her life.

Many odd phobias occur due a negative event occurring at the same time as another event. One client of mine became scared of flying because she found out her grandmother died just before she got on a flight.

In Buddhism, there is an expression *"pain is inevitable, suffering is optional"*. What this means is that negative events are a fact of life. Suffering is what happens when you give a painful event a negative meaning and dwell on it.

Crooked thinking is just a habit, and like biting your nails, you can stop it.

Types of crooked thinking

- Catastrophising: Turning every little problem into a major disaster. This kind of thinking causes your brain to go into fight and flight mode.
- Over-generalising: Saying things like "I always...", "I never..." This kind of thinking makes your brain feel defeated. Why bother trying if the outcome is always or never.
- Exaggerating: Otherwise known as being a drama queen. Some people's brains just love a good bit of drama to add some excitement to the day. They love it so much that they just can't resist adding extra details to every story. There's a fine line between exaggerating and being dishonest.
- Discounting the positive: When something good happens, some people still manage to say something negative.
- Mind reading: Assuming you know what other people are thinking is dangerous and can be destructive in relationships. There are numerous reasons why someone might be grumpy with you; they might be in pain, they might need to go to the bathroom, they may indeed be mad with you, or they may have just realized that they forgot to do something important.

- Predicting the future: If you are a psychic you are allowed to do this one, if not, then how can you possibly know what's going to happen in the future. If you need to predict, be flexible in your thinking.

- Black and white thinking: Thinking that things are totally right or wrong, good or bad. Most things are not either zero percent or one hundred percent.

- Taking things personally: Many things happen in the world that have nothing to do with you; you just happened to be there at the time.

- False cause and effect: Making an assumption that something or someone is the cause of an outcome, without valid information or considering other factors that may be involved.

- Taking the blame and feeling guilty: This is a biggie for moms. While your children share half of your genes (unless they are adopted), and you brought them up with your terrible parenting, they are NOT YOU. As your children get older, you can blame yourself less and less for their failings. You can guide your kids, but you can't control their thoughts, beliefs, attitudes and behaviour; you just can't. You can't change the actions of others directly; you can only influence.

- Not taking responsibility: Things don't just happen to you. You are 100 percent responsible for your thoughts, beliefs, plans and actions. No one has a vested interest in your life the way you do. There are some bad things that will happen to you that are completely out of your control. But, it is you that determines the eventual outcome. For your kids, you also need to take some responsibility, but be realistic. You need to take a high level of responsibility for your one year old, but you can and must take less responsibility for a seventeen year old. It's a hard balance to get right, I admit. Taking too much responsibility for your children can stifle their growth.

- Emotional thinking: This means mistaking feelings for facts. Emotions and feelings can change in a heartbeat. Overly connecting with a feeling can be harmful. For example, if you have a day when you feel sad, it doesn't mean that you are depressed. However, if you over identify with the emotion and begin to say *"I'm depressed,"* you produce more of the neurochemicals associated with depression and it may become a self fulfilling prophesy.

- Name calling: When you say or think something negative about yourself or another person, it has a negative effect on your brain function. It will also affect the level of trust in your relationships.

- Scare mongering: Saying things that create a fear in yourself or another person can be linked to catastrophising and exaggerating. For example: *"If you don't brush your teeth for two minutes they will go black and fall out"*.

- Wishful thinking: This stops you taking personal responsibility and action. Good luck is rarely the reason why people are successful; usually good decisions and positive action are the main ingredients.

- Thinking "win-lose": Do you have the mindset that, in order for you to get something good, someone else has to suffer? This is an ugly yet common way of thinking. The aggressive driver, the pushy soccer mom or the guilt beaten mom; who is convinced her kids will suffer if she goes out and enjoys herself for one night. It is possible to find a solution, to most situations, involving win-win for both parties. The solution might involve active listening, discussion, brainstorming and compromise, but it is there.

- Thinking negative thoughts about someone else: Believe it or not, this one is the most destructive crooked thought pattern of all. Whether you have feelings of hatred, jealousy, blame or resentment, these feelings will fester and harm you from within. Negative thoughts about others are often projections of negative thoughts about yourself that you don't like to admit. When someone does you wrong, you have a decision to make: Let the negative feelings grow inside you OR do something about it and forgive. Practice compassion (everyone makes mistakes and deserves to be happy), acceptance and forgiveness.

The main type of crooked thinking is negative thinking. Daniels Amen describes negative thoughts as "Automatic Negative Thoughts" or ANTS. I love this metaphor because you can learn to crush your ANTs.

I have worked with many children who were negative thinkers, and I would often read them a wonderful children's book: "The Huge Bag of Worries". In the story, Jenny is a little girl who carries around a huge bag, filled with worries. She meets an old lady who teaches her how to deal with her worries. The old lady teaches Jenny to bring her worries out into the open, and share them. Some of the worries disappeared as soon as they came out of the bag, as they "hate the light of day," some belonged to other people and some the old lady dealt with. It is a powerful metaphor. I have combined this story with a model for behaviour change, used in management of children with autism. The exercise will help you notice your patterns of negative thinking and combat them.

Exercise 7.1 Thought Journal

Print the exercise from the workbook or take a page in your journal. Note down any negative thoughts, for at least one day. Every time you notice yourself having a negative thought, follow the steps below:

Step 1. Stop and notice the negative thought. Say it out loud, if you are alone. Then write it down.

Step 2. Identify the type of negative thinking

Step 3. Ask yourself what was the trigger? For example: "I'm saying I'm a looser because I made a silly mistake and I'm tired"

Step 4. Ask yourself out loud and write down the answer to these questions:
- Is it true? What's the evidence? Is there evidence that it is untrue?
- Does the thought really "belong" to me, or is it something everyone thinks from time to time?
- Is there something I could do right now to make the thought go away, for good? If so take positive action. This might include sharing it with someone.

Step 5. Create a positive thought to counteract it. "*I made a silly mistake; everyone does sometimes, I am going to learn from it and try not to do it again*" or "*I shouted at my child because I was angry; I will say sorry and try not to do that again. I need more time to relax, so I am not on edge so often*".

Positive thinking

Positive thinking is the Holy Grail in my opinion, as our thoughts become our reality. If we are seek to find the positive in every situation, we will perceive ourselves as having more happiness, health, wellbeing and success.

Just like negative thinking, positive thinking is a habit which can be strengthened with practice.

There is a new branch of psychology, led by Martin Seligman, author of Flourish. Traditional psychology focuses on reducing suffering and mental illness. In contrast, positive psychology aims to increase wellbeing, which leads to the reduction of suffering and illness.

Exercise 7.2 Positive thinking journal

Every night, for one week, write only positive things in your journal. If you start writing something negative, stop and notice it and allow the negative thought to flow away and think of a positive take on the situation.

If you need some guidance write about:

- Something that made me happy today…
- What went well in my day?
- Something I am grateful for…
- I felt engaged or passionate today when…
- I felt good about myself because…
- I am looking forward to…
- I felt good about achieving…
- Something I did today to enhance my relationships…
- Something went wrong today, but this is what I learnt from it…

Several years ago I came up with a game for my kids. I had noticed some negative thinking creeping in. Yes, I did blame myself at the time, but I did something about it. I have taught this game to hundreds of families, and it can be like magic. It's free and portable. Get in the habit of playing it every night before bed. If your family prays at bedtime, it can be incorporated into prayer.

Exercise7.3 The Happy Game

Here's how it goes, the first time you play:

Parent: *"Hey let's play the Happy Game, Do you want to go first or shall I?"*

Child: *"I don't know how to play!"*

Parent: *"Okay I'll go first. 3 things that have made me happy today. Well, first is being here with you now. That makes me very happy. Second, I felt great when we had dinner together, and you told a funny joke. Third, I felt happy when someone was kind to me in the grocery store today. Now it is your turn."*

The rules:

- Only positive things
- There are no other rules; be playful and flexible.

Be a positive role model

Children model their parent's behavior, more than anyone else's behavior. I remember hearing my four year old say *"that's completely unacceptable."* I wonder where he got that from! Believe me, I know it's hard to be positive, especially when things are difficult at home, but it's well worth practicing being positive with and around your children. If you do say something negative and significant, explain to your child that you could have been more positive. If you notice negative thinking in your child, mention it and model a positive spin, for them. For example your child says *"I suck at basketball"*; you say *"you didn't have a great game but you made a couple of great passes, don't forget you are just learning, practice and you will get better"*.

Teach your child that we all make mistakes: What defines us is how we respond after the mistake. You may chose to blame others, get angry or give up; OR you may chose to take responsibility, own up, say sorry, stay calm and become more determined to prevent the same mistake from happening again. Develop the mantra "there are no mistakes, only opportunities to learn".

Positivity is infectious. Try going out for coffee with a group of friends and being determined to be very positive (be subtle of course and sensitive to the conversation). You can significantly lift other people's mood by being positive.

If you are still struggling with being more positive try this exercise.

Exercise 7.4 Positive role model

Pick a positive friend or family member. Spend time with them, listen more than you speak.

Notice their posture and body movement, their tone of voice, the words they use, and their eye movements. Try and mirror them subtly.

If you can't think of anyone: Try a TV or movie character like Forest Gump.

Stress

Stress is bad for you! According to the American Psychological Association, in 2012 "the USA is on the verge of a stress induced public health crisis." Stress is a significant risk factor in many life-shortening and debilitating diseases, such as heart disease, stroke, cancer and depression. Stress reduces wellbeing, happiness, health and success.

There are always people who will say "but stress is good for you." So let's begin by clarifying what I mean by stress:

- Stress is the emotional and physical reaction to events in life.
- The effects can be appropriate and positive, such as getting more work done.
- However, stress can also trigger inappropriate and negative behaviors, such as getting upset, angry or overwhelmed. It is this negative stress that can harm your health.

For the rest of this section, I am referring to negative stress. Stress is not some vague feeling. When you are stressed, significant and complex changes occur in your body. Here's my "tell it to a 10 year old" explanation of acute stress.

Stages of acute stress

Stage 1: Brain perceives an event as a threat.

Stage 2: Brain sends nervous and hormonal signals within the brain and to the body.

Stage 3: Stress response
- Increased arousal of nervous system and muscles
- Increase heart rate, blood pressure, muscle tension, respiratory rate

- Blood diverted from non-essential areas, such as bowels and sexual organs and suppression of immune system.

Stage 4: Fight, flight or freeze: Fight refers to actively dealing with the threat. Flight refers to escaping from the threat. Freeze refers to shutting down and not reacting, in the hope that the threat will go away.

Stress was essential to our survival when we were cave women. If a hairy mammoth trampled through the camp, mothers needed to respond quickly in order to save their family and themselves. Now I don't know about you, but I am not a cavewoman, and real life threats to my survival do not occur every day. Yet, many of us are chronically stressed. So here's my "tell it to a ten year old" explanation of chronic stress.

Stages of chronic stress

Chronic stress is stress sustained over a long period of time.

Stage 1: Sustained perceived threat.

Stage 2: Brain sends nervous and hormonal signals within the brain and to the body. However, this can't be sustained over long periods, so the brain and endocrine (hormonal) system may become fatigued.

Stage 3: Effects on body and mind

- Chronic arousal of nervous system and muscles. Always looking out for threats, sometimes creating a sense of threat from just a thought. This can lead to chronic pain, exhaustion, poor memory, attention and performance.
- Chronic increase in heart rate, blood pressure, muscle tension, respiratory rate and subsequent chronic health problems such as heart disease, stroke and cancer.
- Bowel problems, sexual dysfunction and immune system problems.

Stage 4: Tendency to over-react to everyday situations: To be argumentative, aggressive, overcautious, overprotective, fearful, passive and to procrastinate and self sabotage. All of which feeds back into Stage 1.

The great news is that you can do a lot to manage your stress. When you learn to manage your stress, your child will benefit too. You will become a better role model, parent more effectively, reduce confrontation in the family and understand your child's stress and help your child manage it better.

Managing stress

There are three main steps in managing stress:

1. Reduce sources of stress,
2. Improve body and brain health so that it can respond appropriately when stressful event occurs,
3. Learn to reduce the impact of stress.

Chapter 6 we considered how to improve physical health.

Sources of stress or "stressors"

Stressors can be internal (coming from your own mind) and external:

- Internal sources of stress include thoughts, feelings, beliefs and attitudes. You can change these, if you want to.
- External sources include people (your children being a major source), things (like taxes) and situations (like children being ill or having to move). These external sources may not be in your control, but the way you to react to them is within your control.

Exercise 7.5 Sources of stress

- In your journal, write a list of your sources of stress in the last week or
- Write every night for a week about your sources of stress that day.

Pay special attention to those internal ones.

Reducing sources of stress

Some sources of stress are within your control. For example: If you are stressed because you have a great deal of uncertainty about money, then complete Exercise 3.1 "Personal Development Plan" for Finances and take action. If you are stressed because you are totally disorganized, keep losing things and forgetting appointments, do some work on time management.

Some sources of stress are not in your control, such as your child getting ill or your partner having to travel with his job. In this situation, it is best to accept that you are not in control of the source but be clear that you are in control of your response. Consider doing some work on negative thoughts or learning some stress management techniques.

Stress Management Techniques

Review Chapter 4: Self-regulation Toolkit, with special attention to things which make you feel less stressed.

If stress is causing you significant health problems or has been going on for a long time, you may need to see your doctor. A short course of medication may give you a boost, until you are in a good place to access other techniques.

Habits

Habits are learned patterns of behavior which are nearly or totally involuntary and unconscious.

In the early stages of a habit development, there is usually a trigger or cause, which led to the behavior. The behavior is usually followed, at least once, by a perceived reward such as attention, feeling happy or relaxed. When behavior is repeated, it becomes automatic: Something you do without thinking.

When a behavior is a habit, it requires little or no conscious thought and minimal brain effort. It is thought that about 40 percent of the tasks we do every day are habits. Can you imagine if we consciously had to think about everything we did like walking, brushing teeth or eating; we'd have little energy for anything else.

In the book "The Power of Habit: Why We Do What We Do in Life and Business", Charles Duhigg, explains that some people use habits to their advantage in an extraordinary way. The multi-medal winning swimmer, Michael Phelps, had a complex pattern of habits he relied on, every day, to maximize his training and performance. His habits allowed him to perform at a high level, even when things went wrong. During one Olympic final, his goggles filled, essentially blinding him. He was able to carry on with the swim, relying on his habits, breaking the world record!

While some habits are useful, like Michael Phelps pre-swim habits, brushing your teeth or putting your shoes on after your socks; others are not so useful. Some habits are minor inconveniences like tapping your feet while you eat. Others are a problematic like biting your nails till the skin bleeds, drinking half a bottle of wine with dinner or eating a bar of chocolate every night.

A habit can become an addiction when there is a physical or psychological need to do the behavior, and physical or mental distress when forced to stop. If you suffer from addiction, please seek the advice of an addiction specialist.

Habits are important for our health. Positive habits are health assets, such when we eat an apple every day, exercise in the morning on Monday, Wednesday and Friday or write a gratitude journal. Negative habits are health liabilities. Just consider the effects of eating a giant cupcake every morning, watching soap-operas for two hours a day or engaging in negative thinking.

One solution to getting rid of a negative habit is:

Step 1. Identify the "bad" habit and its trigger

Step 2. Identify the new "good habit" or behavior

Step 3. Decide on a trigger (it can be the same as the old habit's trigger, or a new one)

Habit development

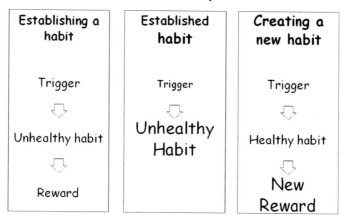

Step 4. Decide on a reward for the new habit

Step 5. Practice 20 – 30 times. NASA research showed that habit formation requires repetition of a new behavior approximately 26 times.

To develop a new positive habit that doesn't replace an old negative one, follow steps 2 to 5.

Exercise 7.6 Developing a Positive Habit

Print the exercise from the workbook or complete the following statements in your journal:

- The habit I want to be rid of is…
- My triggers for the old habit are…
- Why I want to be rid of this habit…
- How my life will be different when I am rid of this habit…
- The new habit I want to develop is…
- My triggers for the new habit will be…
- Why I want this new habit…
- The reward for the new habit will be…
- How my life will be different when I have this new habit…

Step 2: Create an Action Plan and Date to be reviewed…

Step 3: Practice new habit 20 – 30 times. Be consistent.

Step 4: Review progress after 5, 10, 15, 20 times. Are you making progress? If not, consider a new trigger or reward.

When we develop one new positive habit, it becomes easier for us to form other new positive habits. So get started with one, get really good at it, and then add in another. Remember: Once the behavior becomes a habit, you won't need to think about it, and you will do it with minimal amounts of effort and energy.

Self esteem and confidence

Self-esteem is your overall opinion of yourself, your good bits and your bad bits. When you have good self-esteem, you are likely to feel confident and deserving of good treatment.

Beginning in early childhood your self-esteem has been affected by:

- Your relationships and how other people treat you
- Life events and the significance you placed on them
- Illness, disability or injury
- Your culture and religion
- Role and status in society
- Your thoughts, attitudes, beliefs and perceptions
- Low self-esteem can lead to:
- Crooked thinking: Such as saying "I can't" or "I'm not good enough".
- Negative emotions: Such as worry, discouragement and fear.
- Destructive behaviors: Such as passivity, procrastination, self sabotage or taking a back seat.
- Physical effects: Such as stress, tension, clumsiness and fidgeting.
- Low confidence: The ultimate blow.

Six things you should know about confidence

1. Like IQ, confidence is not one thing. You can be very confident about one area of your life but be a wreck about another.
2. Many people who seem to be confident are faking it.
3. Confidence is rarely the starting point. It comes with action, practice, success and learning from failure.
4. People will notice your level of visible level of confidence and treat you accordingly. If you speak or act in a confident way people will think you are confident; they may not think you are right though.
5. Everyone's confidence fluctuates, every day.
6. Sheryl Sandberg, in her book Lean In, urges women have to be a little cautious when it comes to confidence, as it can be perceived as arrogance.

How to be more confident

Here are some ideas to help you become more confident:

- Connect with your authentic self, in particular your values, strengths and passions. When you are connected with your authentic self, you will be more confident.
- Look after your physical health. Looking good and feeling good improve confidence.
- Practice self-regulation techniques such as diaphragmatic breathing.
- Set yourself up to succeed. Make a really good plan and take consistent action.
- Fake it! People who are confident think positive thoughts, like "I'm good at this." They don't pay attention to negative thoughts. Instead, they force themselves to feel and act confidently. After some time, confidence can become an effortless habit.
- Be kind to your mind. Confidence grows when you pay attention to your successes, celebrate them, share them, and wallow in them. Confidence grows when you notice and learn from your mistakes, accept that everyone makes them, forgive yourself and move on.
- Tackle any crooked thinking you might have. In his book Unstoppable Confidence, Kent Sayre recommends changing any negative thinking into a silly voice, like Mickey Mouse. It is hard to take criticism when it comes at you in a cartoon voice. Humor can be a great confidence booster.
- Surround yourself with confident people who make you feel good about yourself and model them.

Look the part: Dress appropriately to the situation, in clothing that you feel comfortable in. Makeup and hairstyle can also be important for confidence. Body language is really important.

Practice standing or sitting confidently. Sit relaxed and back a little, and hold your head held high (imagine someone pulling up on a hair on the crown of your head). Let your arms rest comfortably at your sides; you can hold something if that help, but don't fiddle.

◊ Breathe abdominally.
◊ Give a comfortable level of eye contact, for you and your peers.

- Speak the part: Focus on speaking calmly, clearly and speaking your truth. When alone, practice vocal warm up exercises.
- Playing the part: Practice, practice and then practice some more.
- Do things you are good at. Stop and notice how good you are at them and say out loud "hey, I'm really good at…" even if it's folding laundry or making sandwiches. Not everyone is good at those things.
- Remember Wayne Gretzky's quote: "*You miss 100 percent of the shots you don't take*"? When entering a confidence-challenging situation, ask yourself: "*What is the worst thing that could happen?*", "*What is the best thing that could happen?*" And "*how would I feel to miss out on the best thing that could happen?*"

The following exercise will help you increase your confidence.

Exercise 7.7 Confidence boost

- Identify all of the conditions or situations that make you lack confidence. Do any of them make you feel fearful? Is the fear justified?
- Think back to a time in your life when you were most confident. Imagine vividly. How did you feel? How did you stand? How did you act? How did you think? What did you see, hear, smell and taste?
- Think of something you are good at and a time when you felt successful at this. Say out loud "*I am good at…*" Imagine someone saying to you "*wow you are so good at…*" How would it make you feel, think and act?
- Think of a situation that makes you feel insecure. Think of the person (real or fictional) who would be most confident in this situation. Name them. Think about how they would stand, feel, act and think in that situation. Imagine that you are standing, feeling, acting and thinking like them. Imagine you are confident like this person; how would you deal with the situation now?

Julie's mind

Julie was not in a good state of mind, when she came to see me. She was stressed and engaging in some very destructive crooked thinking, about her self-worth and role as a working mom. Since becoming a mom, she had developed some great habits such as eating together as a family and always eating fruit before dessert; something her children were sticklers for. Many bad habits had crept in: Finishing off the children's food, spending hours on social media and eating a bar of chocolate, whenever she felt stressed or when the family watched TV together. Her self confidence was at an all time low, not helped by feeling that her return to work had been a "disaster". Julie responded very well to the exercises in this chapter, she had the advantage of having been a very positive teen. She was able to see her crooked thinking, for what it was: Just "fleeting thoughts that don't deserve my attention". She found that improved time management reduced much of her stress. Meditation and exercise helped relieve much of what was left. Julie was determined to develop new healthy habits around food and exercise. During our sessions, we often discussed her self confidence, which was slow to improve. A personalized relaxation recording I made for her on self confidence was the turning point. After a month of listening to it daily, she was feeling much more confident. This improved state of mind helped Julie make plans for her future with confidence and determination.

Improving the health of your mind is one of the most effective ways to boost health, happiness and success. Addressing crooked thinking and stress and developing healthy habits and high self confidence are great ways to begin this process.

Chapter 7 Summary

Taking the time to improve the health of your mind will reap enormous benefits.

Giving your children a head start with mind health will benefit them throughout their life and increase their levels of happiness, health and success.

Your subconscious mind is often controlling your behavior, but the information is often incorrect and sometimes harmful.

Crooked or negative thinking is bad for your health, wellbeing and success. It is, however, a habit that can be changed.

Positive thinking is good for your health, wellbeing and success. It is a positive habit that can be developed and internalized.

Negative stress is harmful to health. There are three steps to reducing stress:

- Reduce sources of stress
- Improve body and brain health so that it can respond appropriately when stressful event occurs.
- Learn to reduce the impact of stress

Reducing negative habits and developing new positive habits will help you achieve lasting change

Self-esteem and confidence can help you create the balanced life you deserve and desire.

Chapter 8

RELATIONSHIPS

Our relationships with other people are essential to our wellbeing. A kind word from a loved one can brighten your whole day; a mean word can destroy it. Relationships can affect your health, certainty, performance, habits, self-esteem, mood, brain waves, connectedness, heart rhythm, love, stress levels, expectations, growth, desires, values, goals, purpose, perspective, passion and feeling of contribution and so on.

Like a fragile orchid, relationships need to be nurtured with the right amount and the right kind of attention. When you were a cute baby, people would love you just for your innocent smile, the serenity of your face while you slept, or the way you peed on grandma's favorite rug. When you become an adult, however, you need to work a little harder. It's important to think of the time you spend nurturing your relationships as an investment, one with potentially enormous benefits.

The problem with relationships is that they are so complicated. They are so complicated because we are all so complicated.

Back in chapter 2, we discussed seven facets of authentic self: Personal perspective, values, strengths and weaknesses, passion, needs, purpose and thought patterns. We also discussed how the authentic self is constantly changing and evolving. These facets of authentic self provide the script for your life. Like us, the people around us have their unique script, which is constantly changing and evolving. When we interact with other people there may be conflict between our script and theirs.

Have you ever experienced a time when your child's energy and playfulness has irritated you? Maybe you have a headache and your child is being noisy. In that moment, your child is thinking, "its fun running around in circles, blowing this whistle." You are thinking, "My head hurts and I want to sleep. Why won't he be quiet?" Your child runs round in circles blowing a whistle. You feel irritated, and then shout and snatch the whistle from your child. Your child thinks "mommy is mean and doesn't like me" and starts to cry. You think "great, just what I need: More annoying noise!" Then maybe you shout some more… Many other times you wouldn't have minded your child's behavior, you may have even thought it cute. But in that moment, there was a clash between your thoughts and behavior, and that of the person you love most in the world.

The importance of relationships

Positive relationships are good for all aspects of your wellbeing, and being content with your life is good for your relationships.

If you want to improve an area of your life it helps to seek out and spend time with people, who have what you are seeking. Your behaviors are significantly affected by the people you spend time with. Consider a life asset, such as health or finances, you are probably somewhere near the middle of the five adults you spend most time with. So, if you want to improve your health, consider spending more time with people who lead a healthy lifestyle. If you want to return to work but are worried about coping with work and family, go out for drinks with your friends who work and ask them how they balance their lives.

The rest of this chapter is devoted to nurturing relationships. The aim is to enhance the already healthy ones and improve the unhealthy ones.

Exercise 2.2 "The Wheel of Life" asked you to assess your level of contentment with various life assets including your relationships, in general. This was of course too simplistic. We all have some relationships that help us flourish and others that are like a train wreck. The next exercise will help you evaluate the health of the relationships in your life, right now.

Exercise 8.1 Relationship audit

Step 1: My Relationships

Complete the exercise from the workbook or take fresh page in your journal. Complete the exercise in pencil.

- Draw a small circle or stick figure in the middle, to represent you.
- Add a stick figure and name for each significant relationship. Put the most significant people, close to you and the less significant people near the outside of the page.
- Write as many or as few people as you like. Next to their name, rate your satisfaction with the relationship.

For significant or low-satisfaction relationships, complete the next step.

Step 2: Quality of relationship

- Then think about your relationship with each person. Think then write about that person:
- What do they do for me? Describe the positive and negative. Describe their good bits and their bad bits (think perspective, values, strengths, weaknesses, passion, needs, purpose and behavior)
- What do I do for them? Positive and negative.
- How does this relationship make me feel?
- Overall how important to me is this relationship" (+10 = most important, 0 = not important at all)?
- How much effort do I put into this relationship" (+10 = maximum effort, 0 = no effort at all)?
- What can I do myself, to improve this relationship?" and if so "what actions am I going to take?

I hope this was an enlightening exercise. If you see some relationships are not going well, the next section is for you. Different types of relationships have unique characteristics and dynamics and need to be addressed in different ways.

Relationship types

We are going to focus on three types of relationships, which relate to moms including relationships with:

1. Your child or children
2. Adults
3. Your partner

Your child

As parents, we rarely take the time to consider a vital question: "What is the end-goal of parenting?"

Exercise 8.2 The goal of parenting

In your journal answer the question:

If raising my child was a project, what would be my end-goal?

Of course, parenting is not as simple as most other projects. Parenting is life-long; most parents never stop worrying about and supporting their children, even when they are adults.

For me, the goal of parenting is to raise happy, healthy, well-balanced, ethical, values-driven children who achieve their full potential. For you, it may be something different, but it is important to know what your goal is.

Balanced parenting

It's incredibly difficult to get the balance right, when it comes to parenting. Many moms struggle with questions such as: "Am I too harsh or too lenient", "when should I allow privileges and independence" and "how should I help my child when he is struggling"?

Balanced parenting involves:

1. Creating an environment of unconditional love, certainty, empathy, tolerance, forgiveness, guidance and flexibility.
2. Accepting that your child is unique. They have their own perspective, needs, values, strengths, weaknesses, passions and purpose, even from

an early age. They are NOT YOU and they are not that relative, who turned bad!

3. Being clear that you are the boss. In the early years of parenting, you are in charge. This hierarchical relationship exists for very good reason: Your brain is more developed; you have experienced life; you determine the values system for your family and you have a responsibility to care for and protect your child. As a parent, the buck stops with you. I have seen many families where at times this hierarchy is inappropriately reversed, indeed at times mine has been. Like the tyrannical toddler who won't let his mom finish the grocery shopping without candy, or the teenager who bullies her mom into letting her date an unsuitable boyfriend.

4. Boundary setting is an essential part of parenting. It's not easy, but if you do it well your child will benefit in the future. Keep your end-goal in mind when setting boundaries and aim to be fair, open and consistent. When my children say I am being too strict, I say "sorry you feel that way, but that's my job".

5. Understanding bad behavior. "Bad" behavior in a child is a signal that their needs (health, certainty, love and connection, esteem, growth, contribution) are not being met at their desired level. Such behavior rarely arises from negative intent, at least initially. For example a child who is struggling academically at school may feel uncertain and have low esteem. They may react by becoming clingy and demanding at home (gaining certainty and esteem). If the parent becomes annoyed and frustrated with their child, the feeling of being unloved is added to the equation. So the child ups the ante, becoming clingier or more demanding. They may even add in some shocking behavior. If your child is behaving badly, think about what needs are not being met at the desired level and then look for positive ways to meet them. If your child is old enough, ask them directly.

6. Picking your battles: There may be many things you'd like to change about your child, but if you address too many things at once your child may become overwhelmed, uncertain or hopeless. Consider dealing with the major issues first, when they are resolved, move onto smaller ones. Try "the carrot" approach first, employing "the stick" approach only as a

last resort. Clarify the problem and aim for a collaborative approach to problem solving, if age appropriate.

7. Humility and forgiveness are essential in parenting. We all make mistakes, its part of being human and we all deserve forgiveness. Children when they are young, often idolize parents and think they can do no wrong, and this a very high standard for children to live up to. To help your child developed realistic expectations and a good value system: Acknowledge your mistakes, apologize and show your child that you learn from your mistakes. When your child makes a mistake, forgive them and explain that we all make mistakes; the important thing is to learn from them.

8. Setting realistic expectations: It is easy for parents to set unrealistic expectations. Many set expectations that are too high, like getting straight A's plus excelling at sport and playing a musical instrument. Some children, are motivated by high expectations, they work hard, and achieve great success. Others may fail to meet your standards, despite working hard, leaving them feeling demoralized. Still others will feel overwhelmed and hopeless that they can't reach the standards set, and so give up. There is also danger in setting expectations too low, as this can lead to boredom, lack of direction and poor self motivation. Who said being a parent was easy?

9. Ensuring that everyone gets down-time: Periods of awake-time free from overstimulation and demands are vital. In this fast-paced, technology driven world it is hard for any of us to get adequate down-time. This can be particularly problematic in children and teens: Leading to chronic over-arousal of the brain. In turn, this can lead to bad behavior, stress, exhaustion, burn-out, irritability, anger, mental and physical health problems, poor performance and relationship difficulties.

The two parent family

The relationship triangle between two parents and their child, can be challenging but works best when parents engage in an equal partner relationship together, working as a team, to meet the needs of their child. When parents have shared or complementary parenting styles and common values, purposes and passions, families tend to thrive.

It is normal for one parent is stricter than the other. But, too much disparity can lead to conflict between parents, and between parent and child. Consider having a frank discussion with your partner on your aims for parenting, your values and your rules. Then plan how you will work together. When it comes to parenting, competition and conflict between parents is usually not healthy.

Siblings

Sibling rivalry and animosity are common in many families. Multiple children in a family "compete" to have their needs met. What sibling rivalry boils down to is this: One child perceives that their sibling is having their needs met at a higher level, than they are.

In many families attention, love, time and sometimes more basic needs, such as food and safety are not equally distributed between siblings. Parents often do treat children differently, for all sorts of reasons. For example: If you have one child who works hard and is self motivated, and another who tends to be a bit lazy, then you may be stricter and pushier with the second child.

If one of your children has health problems, special or additional needs, it may not be possible to share time and attention equally between children. Some of these siblings become resilient and develop a nurturing, empathic personality. Others, however, can feel resentful, neglected or angry, and act out to get attention.

Open communication can help reduce sibling rivalry: Acknowledge differences between siblings and reassure each child that you love them for who they are.

A few things should know about teenagers

- The teenage years mark the transition between childhood and adulthood; dependence and independence. Add in the pressures of hormonal changes, relationships with peers, the development of desire for intimate relationships, educational expectations, changing responsibility and impending financial independence and you have the potential for a whole heap of problems.
- The brains of teenagers are still developing; in fact, the frontal lobe doesn't stop until around 25. The frontal lobe is the CEO of the brain.

Its functions include controlling attention, impulsivity, problem solving, empathy, planning, organizing and spatial awareness. Given this fact, I sometimes find it hard to believe that we let kids drive nine years before their brain has fully matured! As a parent, you may often have to compensate for this poorly developed frontal lobe.

- Teenagers are constantly trying out new scripts for their life. They may have a different script for certain settings or different days. One day the script might be "I'm going to work hard. I want to have a good job when I am an adult." The next day the script might be "I can't be bothered to get out of bed. Getting a good job is over-rated. I'll just wait till I win the lottery".

- Teenagers are trying to figure out who they are. Their identity is in a constant state of evolution and flux and may vary between settings.

- Teenagers are astute observers of your flaws, mistakes, and inconsistencies, and they know when you are flaunting your power. Consequently, they may feel you treat them harshly or unfairly, or lack respect for you.

- Many teens are egocentric, ungrateful and impulsive. Developmentally they are beginning to learn how to meet their own needs. Taking responsibility for their own destiny, may feel daunting to a teen. They rarely think about meeting your needs, or about how much you have sacrificed for them. One day they may be grateful and thank you for the amazing job you have done, but don't hold your breath.

- It is normal for the hierarchical relationship between you and your teen to evolve. It may move towards an equal partner relationship, it should not however, be reversed. If teenagers feel disempowered and insignificant, they will seek ways to feel in control and significant, often unconsciously. They may do this by engaging in behavior, they know you will disapprove of. They may become rude, confrontational, violent, and aggressive, get drunk or take drugs. Some become totally disinterested in anything and seem not to care about their future. This seems counterintuitive, but nothing creates fear and feeling of disempowerment, in a parent, like thinking their child is going to be a failure. The natural response of a parent in this situation is to find the cause or to fix things; but this increased attention can reinforce the behavior

- Teenagers need reassurance that they still belong in the family and that you will always love them unconditionally.

- For teens with a chronic illness, physical, developmental or learning disability, the evolution of the parent child relationship is likely to be different, slower or may not ever occur. This can be difficult for a parent, who began with an expectation that their child would mature and become independent. Such parents may suffer a type of grief reaction and acceptance may take many years. Parents of a child with additional needs tend to do better when they have a high level of support.

Adult relationships

Many moms I have worked with describe times of loneliness and isolation. While they might be with their children, every waking hour, they crave adult connection and interaction. Adult relationships can take on many forms. Many moms have multiple adult relationships of varying intensity, closeness and purpose. Sometimes the need for adult connection is met by a partner or family member. Stay-at-home moms often rely on the friendship of other moms. Moms who work have the additional workplace relationships, where often individuals may not understand the competing demands placed on working mothers.

When a new mom has her first child, her relationships with other adults in her life are bound to change. Some relationships will end; others will strengthen. When you are experiencing difficult times, you often discover who your true friends are.

Your partner

Here, we are talking about your husband, spouse or intimate partner. Here are some key markers of "partner" relationships that work well:

- Both partners aim to meet some of each other's needs (health, certainty, love and connection, esteem, growth, contribution), without having to ask or demand.

- Both partners see each other as friends and equal partners. They value collaboration, compromise, shared purpose and vision for their family and spend quality time together. There is no room for competition.

Sharing of obligations varies greatly, but roles are agreed upon, and both partners take responsibility for their role in the relationship.

- It is important that partners have compatible sexual needs and desires. Compromise is often needed when there is an incompatibility. Low sex drive is common in moms of new babies, who are often exhausted, may experience pain on intercourse or may have suffered a difficult delivery. A woman may need to negotiate with her partner, to find a way to meet his sexual needs; he in turn may need to compromise by having more realistic expectations of his partner.
- Avoiding negativity (more on this below).

Partner relationships are significantly altered when children arrive. There can be good effects, like sharing the common love and bond with their child. However, the arrival of a child creates so many additional demands on time, money, energy and attention that it is inevitable that the partner relationship will change. Parenting conflicts, stress, lack of sleep, additional workload in the home and financial concerns are just some of the extra pressures.

Moms, are most commonly the main caregiver for their new baby, often suffer from chronic tiredness and preoccupation with meeting the needs of their child. This is turn can lead to less time, love and attention for their partner, which in turn may take a heavy toll on the relationship. Even though a partner may at first understand this change, if it persists it can lead them to feeling neglected, insignificant, unloved, and unimportant and that the relationship is not working. For families with additional pressures, such as an ill or special needs child, the strain on a relationship can be enormous.

Both partners have to work hard to make the relationship successful. Many relationships end because one partner is unwilling to accept their role in their problems, but it is rare for a relationship breakdown to be totally one-sided.

We all think negative thoughts about other people, from time to time. If this becomes a habit in a relationship, it can be very destructive. When negative thoughts turn into negative communication and behavior, this is a bad sign. The psychologist John Gottman's research on divorce identifies "the Four Horsemen of the Apocalypse". According to Gottman four types of negative interaction are markers of a relationship in crisis: Criticism, contempt, defensiveness and stonewalling. Criticism is a form of pervasive complaint and may involve labeling of character and making someone feel guilty. For example, a man forgets to pick up milk on the way home from work, and his partner says "you are so lazy", when in fact, he's just worked a ten hour day for the family. Contempt, which may come in the form of mean sarcasm, name calling or cynicism, is a sure fire way to make someone feel insignificant. Defensiveness is often a side effect of a long-term negative, critical, blaming relationship and may involve one partner failing to take responsibility for their role in the problem. Stonewalling is disappearing emotionally or physically. Examples include: Refusing to engage in a conversation about an important matter or storming off and leaving the room.

Double bind

Have you ever been in communication, with another person, where you just know you can't win? This is known in psychology as a "double bind." A double bind is a dilemma in communication where one person receives conflicting messages, creating the feeling that they will be wrong regardless of what they do. In addition, the person can't leave the situation. The consequence to that individual is often crooked thinking or undesired behavior.

Sadly the double bind dilemma often occurs in families. It may originate from a clash of perspectives between two family members, or the setting of unrealistic expectations or inconsistent boundaries. This in turn, can lead to feelings of distrust, lack of love and fear.

Here's an example: A parent says to a teen, "You're just a kid. When you live under my roof, you follow my rules". The teen now believes that he is weak and dependent on the parent. Later, the parent says: "Why do you never take responsibility? You need to start pulling your weight." This comment suggests that the parent wants the teen to be mature and independent. Now, the teen feels helpless and trapped by these conflicting messages. He unconsciously finds ways to control the situation by acting out or becoming defiant, or he tries to ease his emotional pain by taking drugs, self harm or running away.

Sometimes moms can feel they are in a double bind with their partner. On one hand, they are dependent on for income and the roof over their head; on the other hand they feel trapped, unhappy or even abused. If you ever feel in a double-bind look for positive ways to deal with the emotional pain such as therapy, exercise or getting a job, to become more independent.

How to improve relationships

There are many thousands of books written by experts, on relationships. My aim is to give you some basic principles to consider regarding your significant relationships. I have developed a three step plan for helping my clients improve their significant relationships, whether it's with a child, a lover or a friend.

Step 1. Understanding the other person.
Step 2. Changing you.
Step 3. Consciously creating a positive relationship

Step 1: Understanding the other person.

The first place to start is to consider the other person. We have established that a common cause of problems is a clash between your life-script and the other person's.

Empathy means understanding another person, especially their intentions and feelings, in a non judgmental way. When we are empathic, we can gain useful information about the other person that will help us understand the relationship. When we act in an empathic way, the other person feels understood and this is a great feeling, for both parties.

Exercise 8.3 In your shoes

Think about the other person your relationship. Imagine you are the other person.

- What is their story and perspective on life?
- What do they value?
- What do they consider to be their strengths?
- What do they consider to be their weaknesses?
- What are their passions?
- What needs drive them? (health, certainty, love and connection, esteem, growth, contribution)

- What do they consider to be their purpose in life?
- What are their thought patterns? Perhaps they are an optimist, a pessimist, a realist or a philosopher?

Put your hand on your heart and imagine you are the other person. Imagine you are putting on their shoes in the morning, ready to leave the house. Imagine what their day will be like. What will challenge them and what will go well? How will they think, feel and behave? What will make them happy and unhappy? What will they feel when they see and interact with you?

The things you have written are your perception and your judgment. It's possible you might be wrong. How accurate do you think you are about the other person? Ask yourself "do I know them well enough to make these judgments." If the answer is "no," then perhaps you need to get to know them better.

Finally, compare their facets of authentic self with yours. Do you see any similarities or differences? If so, what are the consequences?

I hope this exercise has helped you better understand the other person in your relationship. Next, we'll consider you.

Step 2: Changing you.

I don't for one moment believe that you can single-handedly change your relationship. But I do know that that it is difficult to change another person directly. What you can do is influence, by changing your behavior.

Here are some healthy ways to change yourself, in order to strengthen your relationships:

- Take responsibility for your role in the relationship and being determined to do your best to enhance your role. When you fail to take responsibility, blame the other person and make no effort to improve the relationship, you become a powerless victim.
- Bring compassion to yourself. You deserve to be happy, healthy and successful.
- Bring compassion to the other person. They too deserve to be happy, healthy and successful. This doesn't mean you becoming a door-mat or settling for second best. Combine compassion with assertiveness.

- When you are content that your needs are being met, you will be able to meet your partner's needs, at a higher level. It is important to find healthy ways to meet your needs. If your needs are not met within the relationship, you may seek to meet them elsewhere, in healthy or unhealthy ways. Healthy examples: Sarah's need for growth is not being met by being a stay-at-home mom, so she takes a painting class. Jim's need for variety is not met within the home and so he goes to see a concert once a month. Unhealthy, damaging examples: Emily's need for certainty is not met by her husband, so she comfort eats when stressed. Tony's need for esteem and variety is not met by his partner, so he works unnecessarily long hours and frequently goes out drinking and gambling with his friends.

- Actively look for ways to meet your partner's needs. For example: If he is experiencing uncertainty at work, reassure him that things are good at home and that you are there for him. If your teen is feeling down, boost her esteem by reminding her of a time when she excelled.

- Do not rely on children to meet your needs. Children are inherently egocentric, and as they grow, their drive is to become independent from you. If your child does meet your needs, then acknowledge and accept it, but never demand it.

- Notice any crooked or negative thinking about the relationship and attempt to change it (see chapter 7).

The aftermath of change

When you attempt to change your relationship, the other person's reaction may be unpredictable. Keep an open mind and be flexible. Behave consistently and allow time for change to work (at least one month). Sometimes change is so subtle and gradual that we fail to notice it; journaling can help you keep track.

Here are some of the many ways the other person might respond:

- They may fail to notice change or perceive it negatively. Like the husband, who interprets his wife's more loving, attentive behavior as manipulative and scheming. If this is the case, you may need to persevere until they are convinced of your positive intent, or you may need to adapt what you are doing.

- The other person may notice and respond positively either with a change in their behavior or by telling you openly. If this happens, notice and acknowledge that what you are doing is working, and carry on with your good efforts, monitoring progress as you go.

- In some situations, no matter what you do, the other person does not change or changes negatively. If this is the case, it is likely that the problem is mainly on their side, or that the relationship problem is so severe that more radical change is needed. Now it's time to seek outside help like seeing a therapist or a separation expert. Ending the relationship is a last resort and must be given careful thought; once you start taking action to end a relationship it can become like a runaway train. Sadly, though, some relationships are not salvageable.

Step 3: Consciously creating a positive relationship

Here, we will consider two ways to consciously create positive relationships: Creating win-win and establishing effective communication.

Creating Win-Win

I first came across the concept of "winning" and "losing" in relationships, in my Public Health management training and was reminded of it when reading Sean Covey's 7 Habits of Highly Effective Teens. According to this model, there are four types of human interaction. Let's use two people as an example: Person A (that's you) and Person B (a family member). Picture the scene: It's your regular family movie night; you rent a movie, eat popcorn and spend time enjoying each other's company.

- Win-lose. You are struggling to find a movie you all want to watch. You are pushy and don't listen. You choose the movie you want to watch. You win and get what you want. B is unhappy and doesn't enjoy the evening.

- Lose-win. B is just not listening to your opinion and makes the case that your movie taste sucks. B chooses the movie. You don't enjoy the movie and feel grumpy all night. You lose; the B wins.

- Lose-lose: You spend 30 minutes arguing with B about what to watch. You eventually give up, deciding not to bother watching anything. Evening ruined: You both lose.
- Win-win: You negotiate and compromise. B chooses this time; you agree not to complain. Next time you will choose and B agrees not to complain. You agree to one veto each, as part of the deal. B enjoys the movie. You think it was okay, but you enjoyed B's company and he enjoyed yours, which is what counts. You both win.

Sometimes feeling like you have "lost" is more about perception than reality. In the second situation, you could win by choosing to see the positive in the situation: "While I might not enjoy the movie, I am determined to enjoy time with my family."

The win-lose or lose-win scenarios are often seen in sibling relationships, where competition is rife. When seen in adult relationships, they can be very destructive.

Go back to the scenario above. Consider variations: First, you are the parent and B is the other parent. Second, B is your six year old child. Third, B is your 15 year old. What is an appropriate outcome for each scenario, for your family?

Exercise 8.4 Win or lose?
Describe three situations:
- You won; they lost.
- You lost; they won.
- You both lost.
- Was there a way to turn these situations into a win-win?

Establishing effective communication
- Acknowledge the fact that communication is a two-way process, between you and the other person, who has a totally different "script" from you.
- See communication as a method of exchanging information both factual and emotional.

- Be open to learning and growing your communication skills. Effective communication is a learned skill; most of us learn much of it unconsciously but sometimes we can benefit from explicit teaching.
- Speak true to your authentic self with compassion towards the other person.
- Practice self-regulation: Being stressed rarely improves communication. Be calm and focused. If you find your stress levels rising, focus on your breathing and take a few slow, diaphragmatic breaths.
- Communication is more than just the words we use. Types of communication include:
  ◊ Verbal: Words, tone of voice, volume etc
  ◊ Non-verbal: Facial expression, body language, dress etc
  ◊ Visual: Like drawing or showing maps or pictures
  ◊ Written: Handwritten letter, email, text, social media etc.
- Be aware that people interpret communication differently. Be explicit if you are communicating something important.
- Be clear about your aims for communicating. Ask yourself: "What outcome do I want to achieve?" and "Is this realistic?"
- Practice listening, understanding and being empathic. If you are uncertain of how the other person is feeling or the true intention of their communication, ask for clarification. For example: "You seem to be feeling unhappy and angry at the moment. Am I right?"
- Avoid making judgments based on too little information. A furrowed brow or an irritated tone may occur for many reasons; don't assume it is because of you.
- Be flexible and try to offer empowering alternatives to conflict.
- Avoid character attacks, like "you kids today are so lazy." These attacks make the other person question the relationship; and feel misunderstood, confused, alienated and mistrusted. Character attacks often lead to withdrawal or retaliation. Your child might say, "What would you know about being a kid today, you are so old?"
- Look out for giving mixed messages, as this can lead to the double-bind dilemma described earlier.

- In your relationships with your child, and close family members look for ways to:
    ◊ Show unconditional love and connection,
    ◊ Create a sense of certainty,
    ◊ Make them feel important, valued and respected
    ◊ Allow for growth, fun, excitement and adventure.
- Avoid making threats regarding withdrawal of love. The love for your child should be unconditional. Be aware that sometimes children come to think your love is dependent on them behaving in a certain way. For example, in highly academic families, many children come to believe that love is connected mainly to academic performance, and this is often a road to unhappiness and lifelong self doubt.

The Relationship Plan

The following exercise is for those significant relationships, requiring help and attention.

Exercise 8.5 Relationship Plan

The relationship plan is like the personal development plan but with some important additions. Complete the exercise from the workbook or answer these questions:

1. Identify both sides of the relationship. Write for example "the relationship between Frank and ME"
2. The good aspects of this relationship are...
3. I am grateful to this person because...
4. The problem with the relationship is... Be really honest, even if it is painful.
5. My desired long-term outcome for our relationship is...
6. How close am I to the desired outcome?
7. What are the consequences of doing nothing? Now, in one year, five years and ten years?

8. Did the relationship ever match my desired outcome? And if so: What was different in my life then? And: What worked then?

9. How would life be different if our relationship reached my desired outcome?

10. What beliefs do I have about relationships in general? And what beliefs do I have about this relationship?

11. Do I have any habits that are making the relationship worse? If so: Can I overcome them?

12. What did I learn from Exercise 8.1 "Relationship Audit"?

13. What did I learn from Exercise 8.3 "In Your Shoes"?

14. What other significant relationships impact this one?

15. What can I do to have my needs met within or outside of the relationship? (health, certainty, connection and love, esteem, growth, contribution)

16. What can I do to meet the needs of the other person?

17. Do I need a mindset change?

18. Practice compassion. Put your hand on your heart and say out loud "I deserve to be happy, healthy, forgiven and understood". Then say "(name of other person) deserves to be happy, healthy, forgiven and understood"

19. Brainstorm ideas for change.

20. Complete an action plan. For example: "Write my journal what went well and what went badly in the relationship each day, and what I could have done differently; or "plan a 'date night' once a week."

21. Review the change in behavior and the effect on the relationship. What's working and what's not? What do you learn from this?

22. What's next for this relationship?

Julie's relationships

Julie had always had a good relationship with her husband, Max, built on friendship and mutual respect. In their parenting years, the relationship had changed, and Julie had come to take almost total responsibility, for the home and children. While she was not working this had been okay, but her return to work had created a feeling of imbalance. Added to this her exhaustion, feelings of severe overwhelm and dwindling self-esteem; Julie's marriage was under great strain. At times, she felt unsupported by Max, who was non-committal when it came to giving advice. Max, in turn, was feeling a neglected and unloved. Julie's relationship with her children had also suffered: Her eldest was struggling to get homework done, without his mom's supervision; her youngest was acting out, because she missed spending time with mom, and because Julie was so tired, she had become more argumentative with everyone. The exercises in Chapter 1 began to shift Julie's relationships, back to a healthy level, as she became more connected with her authentic self. The exercises in this chapter further improved her relationships with Max and her children. Three revelations were particularly helpful: First, she had not fully appreciated how the stress, caused by her return to work, had made everyone in the family feel uncertain. Second, she and Max had not openly discussed how they felt, for a very long time, so as not to upset one another. Now, was the time for honesty. Third, because her relationships with her family were so important to her, she must make them the cornerstone of future career decisions. Julie and Max committed to a monthly coffee and chat, where they could discuss family life, including their finances. When she returned to work part-time, she had a clear plan of how to protect and improve the relationships within her family.

Relationships are precious and essential to your wellbeing. When they work well, they will support your efforts to create a fabulous, balanced life. When they are troubled, the effects pervade other areas of your life and wellbeing. If you are aware that any relationship needs to be improved, commit to making a plan and devoting some time and attention to change.

Chapter 8 Summary

- Relationships are complex and fragile. They require constant nurturing to keep them healthy.
- Positive relationships are good for all other aspects of your wellbeing.
- When relationships are not working well, you will benefit from exploring the reasons why.

- There are three distinct types of relationships that are significant to you as a mom: With your child or children, with other adults and with your partner.

- It's difficult to get the balance right in parenting. Parenting one child can be complicated by the relationship triangle with the other parent or a sibling.

- The teenage years often present the greatest challenges.

- Your relationship with your partner is likely to change over time and will require ongoing care and attention.

- A three step plan, for improving relationships:

  Setp 1. Understand the other person

  Setp 2. Change you

  Setp 3. Consciously create a positive relationship by creating win-win situations and establishing effective communication

Chapter 9

✑ GROWTH ✑

s adults, we need to feel that we are growing or progressing in our life: It is essential to our wellbeing. The opposite of growth is feeling bored, unfulfilled, under-stimulated, stuck, and uninspired. Lacking growth, we may even feel that life is meaningless.

Yet we rarely recognize growth as it occurs, just like we don't notice the day-to-day growth of our child, until they outgrow their shoes or pants. Even though we can't see it, this sense of growth can be achieved by doing activities which hold a positive meaning for us; that make us feel positive, engaged, challenged, accomplished or that we have mastered something of value.

In the early stages of parenting, you may have felt an intense sense of growth: You have created a new life, a beautiful baby, who you love with all your heart. You may have felt intense pride, connection and happiness. When your baby was small, you were so engaged with meeting her needs: Feeding her, cleaning her, watching her sleep and caring for her. This was probably a steep learning curve, in which you were constantly learning new things.

Over time, however, this sense of growth diminishes for many moms, as parenting becomes routine. The buzz of being a new parent disappears, to be replaced by the roller-coaster ride that is parenting. You begin to realize that your child doesn't need you 24-7 and that one day they may become independent and leave. Your sense of accomplishment and mastery may also diminish as you realize: A mom's job is never done; you can never get things right all the time and your child's destiny is not totally under your control.

Lack of growth can be very harmful. Feeling bored, unchallenged and unfulfilled may lead to depression, addiction, over-parenting or other destructive behaviors. Your child doesn't need you to be their slave, with no life of your own. They need to have a happy, healthy, successful mom, who respects herself and is a good role model. Daughters need to learn that women can have flourishing lives; regardless of their life choices. Sons, the future men of our world, need to learn that women can be capable, strong, creative, productive and significant, while being feminine and caring.

As with most things in life, growth is a balancing act. You can have too much or too little. The bored stay-at-home mom, who ends her exhausting 16 hour day wondering what she has achieved, is an example of too little growth. The single mom, who works two jobs, while studying and managing her family and home with minimal help, is an example of too much growth. I have experienced both too little and too much growth, and both are worth avoiding.

Areas of growth

There are many modalities for growth. You may desire growth in one or multiple areas. Some you may dabble with, others you may seek mastery in.

Personal growth

One great way to feel like you are growing is learning about YOU; otherwise known as personal development, a huge industry of which I am proud to be a part. The type of personal development you engage in depends on what type of person you are, and what you want to achieve. I hope that Chapter 2 gave you a taste for personal growth. There are many books, courses, videos, seminars and webinars, should you wish to pursue the self-directed route. This route requires a high level of self-motivation and discipline to achieve results. If you prefer the group approach, you might want to join a motivational, group coaching program, or a gentler, meditation group. If you need a tailor made approach with personal advice, support and accountability, consider working one-to-one with a coach.

Learning

When you were a child you may have received more learning than you ever desired. Now, as an adult you may enjoy new learning. Your brain is like a muscle; if you exercise it, its' function will improve. Any new learning is good for your brain, as learning new ideas creates new neural networks and keeps existing ones active. Research shows that brain training (new learning and mental stimulation), can protect against this cognitive decline and even Alzheimer's.

As an adult, in the 21st century you can choose to study almost anything that strikes your interest: From astrophysics to appliqué, basketball to baking, craniosacral-therapy to calligraphy. You may decide you want to learn a new skill, which will help you return to your old job, or prepare you for a new career.

You can learn formally by attending an education facility in person or online, or informally with self-directed reading or online courses. The world-wide-web is an extraordinary resource, and there are many ways to learn today, for free.

When you are deciding to spend a significant amount of time, energy and money on new learning, think carefully about what you want to learn. Consider spending five minutes to complete Exercise 3.1 "Personal Development Plan" for "New Learning". Be as specific as possible, with your goals. Ask yourself "is this goal worth the investment of time, energy, money and resources?" Identify the potential benefits. If you begin something only to discover it's not working for you, be sure to figure out why, so that you can learn from your mistake and make a better decision next time.

Creativity

Creativity is an excellent way to achieve growth, and may produce some wonderful by-products. Examples include art, writing, inventing, music, crafts, garden design, dance, cooking and photography. Taking a course in your area of interest is a great way to develop your interest and meet people, who share your passion. Explore local colleges, community centers or online resources such as Udemy and Coursera.

Career

Having a career can be a good way to achieve growth. Many moms miss working when they take a break, to raise their children. Along with missing the growth a career provides, they may miss the social interaction, engagement in a task, sense of purpose, the sense of accomplishment and of course the income. Having a career can increase your level of financial security, long term career development, esteem and sense of variety and contribution outside of the family. Chapter 10 covers career in much more detail.

Relationships

Growth occurs in relationships that are new or developing positively. Examples include: a new friendship, with someone in your yoga class, who will encourage you to attend; helping your child learn a new language, or starting to date again after a bitter divorce.

Financial growth

Financial growth can be very empowering. If you are a mom who hasn't worked for years, relying on your husband for every little expense, getting your first pay-check may bring an immense sense of accomplishment and freedom. You can put the money, you earn, to good use in a variety of ways: From contributing to the family purse, to treating yourself to a new outfit, through to saving for your child's education. Chapter 11 will help you with ways to achieve financial growth.

Health

Taking control of your health can give you an enormous sense of growth. Remember health is your greatest asset. It can begin simply, by doing some research on a health problem or starting a new healthy eating plan, and extend to running your first 10k or having tennis lessons. The added benefit is that, as well as growing you will also be improving your health and maybe even extending your life: Win-win!

Spiritual growth

For me, spirituality is about discovering the essence of life and connecting with your authentic self, with individuals, community, nature or religion, at a deep level.

Spirituality involves setting aside purely materialistic values such as wealth and putting value on qualities such as love, compassion, patience, tolerance, forgiveness, contentment, responsibility, harmony, and contribution. In the case of religious spirituality, there is also a belief in a higher being or beings.

Leading a spiritual life can be good for your health, make you feel connected, give positive meaning to life and create a high level of engagement.

If you are religious, spiritual growth may be achieved by increased involvement in religious practice or by engaging in service work, on behalf of your religious organization.

If you are spiritual but not religious, spiritual growth may be achieved through many outlets such as reading about spirituality, learning to meditate and charity work. The wonderful book *"Beyond Religion"* by the Dalai Lama, is a great place to start.

Lifestyle and Home

Your lifestyle and home can be a great source of growth. Joining a gardening club, taking walks in nature, or improving your home and garden, may fill you with joy and satisfaction. Lifestyle and home are further discussed in Chapter 13.

Community

Maybe you love being active in your community, connecting with people and working towards a common goal, like planting a community garden or serving in a soup kitchen. This can give a sense of much higher purpose and accomplishment. You may want to combine working in the community with something you are passionate about, like special needs children or with something related to your old or future career (win-win). Doing a good deed for another person or cause is good for your brain and overall health.

Lack of growth

Have you ever felt bored, uninteresting, frustrated, unsuccessful or underappreciated? I know I have. This is how a lack of growth feels, and sadly it is a common but slowly, destructive problem for moms. It can breed resentment, dissatisfaction, low self-esteem, lack of motivation and desperation. From a brain perspective, a lack growth may be accompanied by under-arousal of the brain and a feeling of "brain fog". If sustained it may cause cognitive decline, as new neural networks are not being formed. Lack of growth, is undeniably bad for you.

Mommy Brain

There's no denying it: Most moms, at some stage, feel like they are not as mentally sharp as they used to be. For many of us, this is somewhat of a dramatic understatement! There is mixed scientific evidence of the effects of motherhood on the brain. But it can't be denied that many moms suffer from sleep deprivation, low mood, chronic stress and anxiety, all of which do affect brain function. Staying mentally active and experiencing the positive emotions associated with growth, have a protective effect on the brain.

Exercise 9.1 Creating Growth

If you were completing a wheel of life today, what score would you give yourself for growth (out of 10, 10 = maximum)?

What is a realistic satisfaction score for growth to achieve in the next 6 months?

For each of the following types of personal growth, note your current level of satisfaction, your desired level, ways you have achieved growth in the past and ideas for how you could achieve growth in the next six months.

- Personal growth
- Learning
- Creativity
- Career
- Relationships
- Financial growth

- Health
- Spiritual growth
- Lifestyle and Home
- Community
- Other

If you now feel inspired complete Exercise 3.1 "Personal Development Plan", for Growth.

Growth and your children

You are your child's number one role model, for growth. If they witness you value your personal growth, they are more likely to become an adult who values their own growth, at all life stages; even when they are busy with work and family.

I have worked with many moms, who struggle to get their kids to do homework. The problem with homework, often comes down to this: After a long day of being forced to work and "grow" academically, creatively, socially and health-wise (with sports and health education); a child returns to the safety of home, only to be forced to do more work. This can feel like way too much, undesired growth. If you have a kid like this, try working on your area of growth while they do homework. If your child is an independent student tell him "while you are do your homework, I am also going to be working on…" If you have a younger child, or a reluctant student, aim to be in the same room, doing your work; offering advice only when needed. Helicopter moms are so last season!

Chapter 9 Summary

Feeling bored, unfulfilled, under-stimulated, stuck, uninspired or that our life is meaningless is bad for you.

Adults need to feel that they are growing: it essential to health and wellbeing, especially brain health.

There are many modalities for growth and they include personal growth, learning, creativity, career, relationships, financial growth, health, spiritual, lifestyle, home and community.

Valuing and pursuing personal growth will encourage your children to do the same.

Chapter 10

CAREER

*P*erhaps you are one of the lucky ones, who is completely satisfied with your career path? Sadly many moms are not. If you are less than satisfied with your career, this chapter is for you.

At the outset, I'd like to make very clear that being a mom involves a lot of work. Whether you are a full-time stay-at-home mom, a mom who works part-time or you work full time the effort and time involved in managing your family and home is considerable. In this chapter, the terms "work" and "career" will refer to work outside of looking after your family and home.

When it comes to question of "should I work?" there is no right or wrong answer. Some moms have no choice: They either have to work or they have to stay at home. For those moms who do have options, there are many considerations: Your children, your support network, your partner (if you have one), the type of job and the economy, to name a few. Some of these will be within your control; others will be totally beyond your control. Remember though, that you always have the power to make the best of your current career situation.

There are 3 groups of moms I'd like to consider in this chapter:

1. Mom's who work but are not entirely satisfied with what they are doing or with their work-life balance.
2. Mom's who are considering going back to work, ever.
3. Mom's who plan to remain stay-at-home moms, who want to be more content with their situation.

1. Mom's who work

According to the National Association of Child Care Resource and Referral Agencies 71% of women with dependent children were working in 2012, in the USA. In the UK, in 2011 66% of mothers were working (ONS). Sadly many of these women were under-employed (doing a job below their ability), under-paid, unhappy or stressed about their work. Being a working mom brings considerable additional pressures and achieving work-life balance can be difficult.

Some moms take only a short break when they have children; an excellent decision for some. They have good childcare and help in the home, their employer is understanding, and their career progresses as planned. For other moms, returning to work is a disaster.

Some moms take a planned, extended break, returning to work after months or years. Some are forced into a particular job because they need money and it's all they can get. For many moms returning to their pre-child job is not an option because their skills are not up to date, their job has changed dramatically or it's no longer practical.

Moms are the masters of career reinvention. Sandberg's quote about careers being like jungle gyms is a great metaphor for this. Personally, I have had seven different jobs since becoming a mom.

This chapter will guide you through a process of exploring your current career situation and taking steps to create a career that will bring you more happiness, health, success and wealth.

2. Moms who are considering going back to work

To work or not to work? That is the question; the BIG QUESTION!

Even if you are thinking of maybe returning to work in ten years time, it is never too early to prepare. In this fast paced, high-tech world, skills and expertise are changing rapidly. You might make a decision to not worry about this now.

That is fine, but please know that filling the skills gap gets harder, the longer you leave it.

Going back to work is a big decision and it's not to be entered into lightly. As I write this book, the "crystal ball" has not yet been invented, so returning to work requires a big leap of faith. There are many things to be considered in the decision and sometimes you have to give it a go and monitor the effects.

3. Moms who stay at home

If you have no plans to return to work you may want to skip or skim read the first part of this chapter and fast forward to "the art of being a happy, healthy successful staying-at-home mom".

My career experience

I love working. I miss it when I am not working and feel a rapid loss identity, certainty, significance, variety, growth, connection and contribution. You could say I am a work addict! In the last 15 years, I have made the decision to return to work several times, all with greater or lesser success. Another time I decided at the last moment to stay at home, at the last moment.

I have had several periods of being a stay-at-home mom: The first time was when my eldest son was five months old. My plan began at my first antenatal scan. My baby was booked into a well researched nursery six months before he was born. It all went smoothly, until Friday night of my first week back, when my son became ill with a virus. The nine months that followed were a nightmare. My son lurched from one illness to another, culminating in a nearly fatal illness. I missed many weeks of work, and I felt like a total failure, at everything. I then had my first taste of Life Coaching. I saw a coach, who helped me make the very difficult decision, to leave medicine, temporarily and become a babysitter. The cries from my colleagues, friends and some family members of "but all that training and money, wasted?" were deafening.

My next return to work was to work as a teacher's assistant at my sons' school. I loved some aspects of this job: I was very close to my sons, I was helping children learn, work stopped when I left school and it was very sociable. However, I felt bored and undervalued (totally my issue, it's a great job). At the same time as working as a teacher's assistant I trained part-time as a counselor and life coach. I then went on to run a coaching business, specializing helping parents of children with special needs.

During this time, I coached myself extensively and decided to return to medicine, as a Developmental Pediatrician (Community Paediatrician in UK). I researched the role, dusted off my resume and practiced my interview skills. I knew I was the only applicant; I was adequately qualified and well prepared for the interview. The night before the interview I felt uneasy; something felt wrong. I felt a mixture of excited anticipation and dread (pretty normal I know). I had a conversation with my husband, explained my concerns, and he said "I think it's not the right time". I felt huge relief at my concerns being validated. So the next morning, I apologetically turned down the interview. It turned out to be one of my best decisions, ever. What followed was a serious problem with one of my sons. Had I been working, would have felt terrible guilt and regret at having returned to work. I was glad I had trusted my instinct.

Two years later the timing was right: I accepted a role as a Developmental Pediatrician. I loved the job, despite frequently complaining about the limitations of the medical model for special needs kids and National Health Service politics. I had a great babysitter, who made this return to work run very smoothly (thanks Sue!) I would still be in that role had it not been for my family's move to the USA, with my husband's job.

Six months into our move my husband asked "so what are you going to do with your life?" My reply "well since you ask: I want to train in Neurofeedback and return to coaching" and so I set up my business. Running my own business has been fun and an incredibly steep learning curve. However, there was a high cost to running an office and a business that involved mainly working after-school hour: I rarely saw my boys and earned less than my babysitter. A forced, temporary shut-down of my business, due to the immigration process gave me time to re-evaluate again. While I was unable to work, I studied, coached myself and wrote an e-book on test anxiety. I discovered a new love and passion for writing. So to my current career choice: Work at home mom, author, coach and speaker and the highest levels of happiness, health and success I have felt in my adult life.

Each time I have reinvented myself it has been difficult. I feel like a chameleon, ever changing my skin. Friends and family joke with me "what are you up to now?" My evolution has been necessary and I have made many wrong turns. I have learned from the mistakes and am more resilient because of them.

How to decide whether to return to work, change job or career or give up working.

The career flow chart will guide you through the process outlined in this chapter.

Career Flow Chart

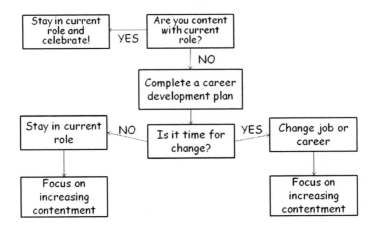

Completing a career audit will help you answer the sometimes difficult question: "Am I content with my current situation?"

Exercise 10.1 Career Audit

Complete the exercise from the workbook or write in your journal:

Step 1. My current role, job or career situation is...

Step 2. Score your current role for its level of meeting the following criteria. 0 = doesn't meet criteria at all; 10 = meets it at the highest level.

Step 3. Score your desired level of meeting each criterion.

Step 4. Star your top five most important criteria for you, when it comes to assessing your role.

- Job security
- Financial security
- Level of interest, fun or excitement
- Level of passion and purpose felt for the role
- Ability to meet my needs in this role
- Ability to meet my child's needs
- Ability to meet partner's needs
- Ability to cope with household
- Level of significance, value and importance you feel
- Quality of relationships within role
- Level of growth felt
- Level of contribution felt
- Matches level of skills and expertise
- Net income/ time ratio
- Opportunity for career development
- Has a positive effect on my health
- Lifestyle afforded by the role
- Fits with my value system
- Role works to my strengths
- I look forward to each day in this role
- This role is stress-free
- Other (insert own)
- Overall contentment

Having completed the audit, review your results. If your top five important criteria are being met at a low level, it may be time to consider a change. If you have a low score for any criteria, which are unimportant to you, at the moment, don't worry.

How to change job or return to work

The important decisions of whether to change jobs or return to work, deserve careful consideration. Believe me you want to do everything you can to make sure it's the right decision. Making the wrong decision can be very harmful to your family, your career and your health.

I'm going to let you into a secret. It's okay to design your career so that it will make you more happy, healthy and successful. Your loved ones will benefit from your increased wellbeing. It's win-win.

It can be a lonely decision to make, so it often helps to run your ideas past other people. It's essential you ask the opinion of your family and take this into account, but be aware they are not in a position to give impartial advice. This is when you might want to consider the help of an expert such as a Coach. Don't assume you know what other people think, ask them. Ask all of the important people in your life "I'm thinking about going back to work, what do you think?", then listen to the answers with an open mind. Remember people have all sorts of reasons for their opinion, take on board what they say but filter it. Beware of asking certain people if you KNOW you are not going to like the answer. Children can often have amazing insights when asked BIG questions, just remember they can be egocentric.

Exercise 10.2 Career Development Plan

Complete Exercise 3.1 Personal Development Plan for Career Change.

Close your eyes for a few minutes and imagine being in your perfect job. Consider what you will have to do in order to be ready for your perfect job? What will your work life be like? How will it affect your family and social life? How will you benefit and what will be the costs?

Leave the question "What's stopping me from achieving my outcome?" exercise 10.3 will help you answer this.

The pros and cons of being a working mom

As with most decisions in life there are positives and negatives to be considered. The pros and cons may be more extreme, if you plan to work fulltime.

Exercise 10.3 Pros and Cons of working

Before you read the next section take two fresh facing pages in your journal. At the top of the left page write "PROS" and on the right page "CONS". Go through the section below writing down all of the pros and cons you can think of. My list is not exhaustive; you may have some of your own.

Add the pros and cons to your Career Development Plan.

Potential pros of being a working mom

Please note; these are just potential pros. Sometimes moms go back to work only to realize they are left with a no net income, they don't get on with their colleagues or there is a negative impact on their children. But get it right and these are some of the potential benefits.

Compensation

One of the main reasons why most people work is income and other benefits, such as health insurance. Income allows you to meet your own needs and those of your family. With more income, your family can afford things that can improve quality of life now and in the future.

Good for your mental health

Working can be good for your mental health. A recent Gallup Poll showed that stay-at-home moms had greater levels of worry, sadness, stress, anger and depression than employed moms. These findings were most pronounced in low income families. This is of course a gross generalization. If your needs (for health, certainty, love and connection, esteem, growth and contribution), are being met at a low level by staying at home consider how they would be met if you went back to work.

Interaction with adults

Many stay-at-home moms say there are times when they feel isolated. No matter how much effort you make to socialize; long days stuck at home with your kids can feel very lonely, no matter how lovely and entertaining your kids are. You may also yearn for conversations that don't involve school grades and activities or ideas for how to get your kids to eat broccoli.

Sense of identity

For many women, sense of identity is closely linked to work. Many moms struggle with a lost sense of identity, when they give up work. I reached a point where I defined myself as "an overweight, tired wife and a mother of two." This realization shocked me, and this negative self image reduced my self-esteem and made me feel worthless. For many moms working or doing something of value, outside the home, can rapidly improve sense of identity and self-esteem.

Sense of achievement

Often a sense of achievement comes with completing a task. For many moms, being a parent is much like being King Canute, ordering the tide to halt and not wet his feet. We may feel powerless against the tide of mess and chaos that is most family homes. Many moms complain of a feeling like they achieved nothing, at the end of each day. Of course raising happy, healthy, successful children is a huge achievement, but it can be hard to keep sight of this. I remember ending my first day as a teacher's assistant feeling a great sense of achievement: I had created a wonderful display in the classroom on the Romans; it was the first time in a long time that I could step back with a sense of pride and say "I did that!" It may also be a long time since you used your skills, felt truly valued or a sense of pride for a job well done.

Personal Growth and Intellectual stimulation

For many moms, staying at home doesn't provide that feeling of personal growth or intellectual stimulation, they desire. The right job can do both.

New challenge

While you know that you can do the job of being mom; returning to work can be an exciting new challenge. New challenges keep our brain stimulated, even when we are not successful.

Positive role model

There is conflicting evidence of whether mom working has positive or negative effects on the outcome for their children. What is clear is that when a mom has a job she likes, her family is financially secure, and she copes well with her various roles: She will be a good role model for her children. In return children may show increased academic performance, resilience and independence.

An investment in your future

You may be considering taking a job, which is not your perfect job, as a stepping stone to a future career. It may improve your resume, self confidence, skills and expertise, prove that your brain still works, improve your interpersonal skills and it will make it easier to make the next career move.

Many women want to safeguard themselves against a family crisis. Not to be a scaremonger but consider scenarios like "what if my husband dies or leaves me?" You may also want to safeguard yourself against "empty nest" syndrome.

Contributing to the family

In many relationships, there is a need for equality in contribution both financially and in work and effort. Many men feel enormous pressure being the only bread winner; they worry about losing their job or getting ill. Having a wife that works may ease this pressure.

Contributing beyond your family

Working is one way to feel that you are contributing beyond yourself and your family. It's good to feel that your work can have a positive impact on other people or a business.

Potential cons of being a working mom

I'm going to address the cons and at the same time begin to offer solutions to overcome them.

Time

Time of course is limited. You only have a set number of hours in any day when you can accomplish tasks. Returning to work may mean that you don't have adequate time for your other roles of being a mother, housekeeper, friend, wife or lover.

Solution: Plan ahead; see Chapter 5, for advice on time management, if you are not a super-mom who can do this alone.

Conflicts with being a mother

Work not only takes up your time but also your energy, focus and drive, away from your children. There may be times when you have to decide between family commitments and a work event. How will you feel if you miss a big development like your child learning to ride their bike or their first soccer goal? Your child may feel like you don't care about them as much (this usually passes).

Solution: Plan ahead. Make a list of all of the conflicts you think you may have. Consider deciding in advice, which compromises you are willing to make. For example: "I can miss Parent-Teacher Association meetings but I will not miss graduation."

Effect on your child

You may worry that working may have a negative effect on your child, especially if it's new to them. Children can start acting out, becoming upset, having trouble with school or homework.

Solution: Be proactive. With good insight into your child's emotional state and your family situation, you can plan to reduce the effect on your child. Remember you are the adult; it's your responsibility to decide what is best for your family.

Depending on their age, you may want to sit down with them. Explain honestly and explicitly:

- That you always love them and you like being with them.
- Your reasons for returning to work (be positive), for example, if you desperately need the money you might say "I think our family would benefit from having more money". Avoid making them feel "scarcity"; this causes stress.
- That you'd love their input into how you can make the situation work "I'd love any ideas you have on how we can have some quality time together".

Plan quality time with your child. Listen non-judgmentally when they talk about the effect it has on them: Tell them that you understand, that you are sorry (I'm a great believer in humility) and try and come up with a solution, together.

Conflicts with being a wife

Many men are happy for their partner to return to work and contribute to the family income; but some are not. Your partner may have a traditional view that moms should stay at home, or he may feel threatened: Thinking that you won't need him, that you won't have time for him or that you will meet someone else at work.

Solution: Be very compassionate to your partner's needs. Take time to let him know he is still significant to you, that you are still there for him, that you can still have fun together, that you still love him, including on an intimate level. Find opportunities to have fun and grow together. This is not easy; it will take focus and planning but it is essential to protecting the health of your relationship.

Managing the home

With less time and energy for managing the home, it can become quite challenging.

Solution: It's time to get super organized, change your standards or outsource. Training other family members to take on mundane tasks will free up your time, teach them independence skills and make them appreciate you more.

Obligation to others

When you are a full time mom your obligation is to your family. When you work you make an obligation of time, energy and productivity to your employer, this may be difficult to adapt to. It is likely that you will no longer be able to be at home in the school vacations, and if your child is sick, what then? Your employer will probably make more demands on your time and energy than you expect.

Solution: Think ahead and plan how you will manage this. Work on accepting this new obligation, after all your employer is paying you for it.

Increased family stress

Working can both cause and relieve stress. Naturally, just like family life, work life can be stressful at times. It is likely that if the cons far outweigh the pros, working will be stressful. The effect depends also on your ability to prevent, recognize and manage stress, all of which skills can be learned. Stress can is harmful to health, wellbeing and performance so must be taken seriously.

Solution: Keep a close eye on your stress. Review the techniques you learned in Chapter 4. Schedule self-regulation time, during your day. You absolutely must do this, if you do not the effects will be much harder to overcome.

Costs of working

The financial costs of working must be taken into account. These include childcare, travel, clothing and of course taxes. It can be very disheartening to realize that you are earning less than your babysitter or actually losing money by working, even if it is part of a longer term plan.

Solution: Plan and research carefully. Sit down and estimate all of the costs. It is likely that you will underestimate by at least 20%. Calculate your hourly rate. Then decide is it worth it. I have worked with women who decide it is worth earning next to nothing because they enjoy working, they want the additional benefits of the job or they see it as an investment in their future. If, however, your main reason for working is to meet an urgent financial need, and you are not earning enough to warrant all of the cons; you need to think again, and search for an option which will be financially worthwhile.

Effect on social life and time with extended family

It is likely that you will have less time for socializing, when you work. You may miss your weekly coffee with a friend, being able to go to a talk at the library or being able to connect with family.

Solution: Planning and prioritizing are vitally important. Using your needs profile, is a good way to prioritize. If you are not sure whether to go to a social event, ask yourself "will this event meet any of my needs at a high level?" If the answer is "no", politely decline. This is not being selfish; it's being sensible. Perhaps arrange a monthly night out with close friends and schedule family calls on your day off.

The need to find childcare

Until your child is old enough to be completely responsible for himself, both legally and practically, you are going to need childcare. Clearly getting childcare right is extremely important for your peace of mind and the health and wellbeing of your child. The type you choose depends on your finances, family situation, role and responsibilities, travel to or with the job, the flexibility of the job and your child's age, stage of education, maturity and personality.

Solution: There is a comprehensive list of the pros and cons of different types of childcare at www.beyondsoccermom/childcare. Go through this list and decide on your preferred option, then take action.

Mindset

Clearly your mindset about returning to work can be a help or a hindrance. Doubt, guilt and regret are common and unavoidable: So deal with them! If you don't really want to work for any reason or if you lack the confidence, mindset may be a significant barrier. Any negative thinking may lead to: Self sabotage when job seeking and poor performance and dissatisfaction, in any job you take.

Solution: Read Chapter 7 Healthy Mind.

Change of status and stigma

When you return to work you leave behind "stay-at-home mom" and become a "mom who works". Consider how you will feel about this and what will others say. In some cultures, communities or towns there may be a negative perception of moms who work.

Solution: Deal with your own feelings and avoid using other people's perception as an excuse, for your own negative thinking. Other people will always have an opinion. Some may upset or offend you about your decision: Some due to jealousy; others due their belief that moms should be at home. Some may have an extreme view; but most will be in between.

Be ready for comments, with a scripted answer. For example "I loved being at home with my kids, but I've decided it's best for the whole family if I work, and now feels like the right time!" Get it in early before anyone offends you and be strong and clear about your intent.

How to decide what job or career to do

If you have decided to return to work or change career, your next decision is "what job or career will I do". This has two important components: The type of work and the method of working.

For some moms, the decision is simple: Return to their before-child job or career. For others, it is more complicated. Challenges include:

- A geographical move that makes it hard to return to your previous work.
- An occupation that has changed so much, that it would require considerable retraining.
- A job incompatible with your family life (like impossible commute, inflexible hours or lots of travel)
- You hated the job, or were never good at it and would never consider going back to it.

According to a 2012 Harvard Business Review article, when we are thinking about what job to do you need to consider three things: your passion, your skills and the market. If you find a job, which meets three criteria it is likely to help you flourish.

Exercise 10.4 The right job

Step 1. Complete the exercise or write in your journal.

Step 2. Describe your family situation in relation to your ability to work

Step 3. Job history: Take two pages in your journal. List briefly all of your previous jobs on the left of the page. Then, on the right side note down all of the things you liked and didn't like about each.

Step 4. List your:
- Strengths, skills and expertise
- Weaknesses and types of work you do not excel at
- Passions
- Values
- Compromises you are willing to make
- Compromises you are NOT willing to make

Step 5. Ask yourself:
- If I won the lottery today, after the long vacation, what would I do?"
- What would I do if I knew I couldn't fail at anything?"

- Do I prefer to work with people or alone?"
- Do I prefer to work in a big organization or a small team?"
- What things do I like about working?"
- What things do dislike about working?"
- What careers do I wish I had followed?"
- How much money I NEED to earn?"

Step 6. Brainstorm on a fresh page write down all of the possible job options you can think of: Even the silly ones. Your "old" job may come to mind, but you will likely have many other ideas. Write until you run out of ideas. Then go through each idea and think about the 16 questions you have just answered. Put a big cross through any job that now seems like it wouldn't work for you.

Step 7. Make a shortlist of all of the jobs that now seem possible for you.

Research

Research the job market. Using your short list go online and look for jobs: Type into a search engine "Find a job as a lion tamer" or "salary for lion tamer". Bookmark interesting pages or take notes in your journal. Have a look at least 20 jobs in your area and note:

- Do you meet the requirements, for the role?
- What does the job involve?
- What types of working arrangements are available?
- What types of salary or compensation package can you expect?

While you are researching, you may have more ideas, add them to your brainstorming list and go through the process for each one.

Networking virtually (example: LinkedIn) or in person can be a good way to find out more, about potential jobs or career routes.

It is important at this stage that you take a very large dose of "realism". It is highly unlikely, maybe even impossible to meet all of your criteria; it is essential to be clear on the compromises you are willing to make.

Types of working arrangements

Full time employee

Advantages: Better pay and benefits, more respect, continuity, ability to get engrossed in the job and feel a sense of accomplishment and belonging.

Disadvantages: Less time with family, freedom and flexibility.

Part time employee

The definition of the number of hours varies between countries but less than 35 hours is usually considered part-time.

Advantages: More time for family and other commitments, enhance resume, ease yourself back into work, and may open doors to full time opportunities, reference for your next job.

Disadvantages: Less pay and benefits, less respect in workplace, difficult to achieve momentum, often end up working more hours than you get paid for, less chance of promotion.

Business owner or entrepreneur

Advantages: Follow your passion and own ideas, set your own agenda, work flexibly, independence, the sky is the limit financially.

Disadvantages: Responsibility, long set up period before you can make money, hard to keep focused, can be lonely, you might have to do lots of tasks you are not good at, high risk financially.

If you have some of the following qualities, you might make a good entrepreneur:

- Creative
- A big picture thinker
- An excellent communicator
- A strong leader, able to delegate
- Risk taker
- Action orientated
- Brave
- Self-motivated

- Values driven
- Energetic
- Self-confident
- Competitive
- Efficient and organized
- Doggedly persistent

Franchisee

The lower risk version of setting up a business is becoming a franchisee or multi-level marketer.

Advantages: Set up costs may begin as low as $5, model is proven, usually the franchise comes with marketing, sales materials and a website, work as hard as you like, choose your hours, possibility of progression within the company, and benefits, if you are a top performer.

Disadvantages: Product may be hard to sell, low income initially, may be a saturated market.

If you are considering buying into a franchise, research carefully. Choose a product you believe in and trust and a company with an honest track record.

Contractor or freelancer

This is working for a company, not as a regular employee. You may be employed for a project or service.

Advantages: Flexibility on the work you choose, pay usually higher per hour, variety of clients and possibility of remote working.

Disadvantages: Poor job and financial security, no additional benefits and constant need to seek new clients and you will have to set up as a business entity (legal and tax implications).

Flexible working

Flexible working is on the increase. It can work for fulltime or part-time work.

Advantages: Flexibility to suit your situation. For example, you may be able to work 8 a.m. to 2 p.m. when your children are at school, and 9 a.m. to 3 p.m. during school vacations.

Disadvantages: Flexible working is still rare and flexibility is often abused or resented. It is important that you are extremely clear about the rules of flexible working at the outset. Flexible working does not mean you can work when it suits you, or that your boss can expect you to work whenever she clicks her fingers.

Remote working

There are an increasing number of companies that work largely or totally remotely.

Advantages: You work at home and can be "around" for your child, you can work in your pajamas, no travel time and you might even be able to work while on vacation.

Disadvantages: Can be lonely, pay may be less, and you might find it difficult to do a focus on the work, with distractions of home and family.

Software exists that allows employers to check what you are spending your time doing. This may seem like "big brother", and it is. However, it allows employers check that employees are actually working and develop trust. Tim Ferris's book "The Four Hour Workweek", offers a guide to how you can switch to remote working, as an employee or entrepreneur.

Temporary work

Advantages: A good way to try out a job or get back into the workforce, without a big commitment.

Disadvantages: Poor pay and benefits, unpredictable and unreliable and may be difficult to arrange childcare, at short notice.

Interim position or internship

Advantages: A good boost for your resume, get experience in a new role and road test the employer.

Disadvantages: Low or no pay, you may be treated poorly and may not lead to a job.

Job sharing

Advantages: Work part-time, share the role and may receive employee benefits.

Disadvantages: Can be tricky to get the dynamic right. This depends very much on the job and your relationships with the other person.

Timing your change in role

Let's face it the timing is never going to be perfect, at some stage you are going to have to bite the bullet and say to yourself: "The timing is good enough". The "good enough" time for you, will depend on: You, your children, your family situation, the job market and other factors. Sometimes fate seems to lend a hand. You may be thinking about returning to work, when a friend tells you of a job opportunity that is too good to miss. You may decide that the timing is "good enough" and plunge right in, or dip your toe in the water and ease yourself in slowly by taking a part time job. It is worse to regret not having tried something new; than to be brave enough to try and it not work out. If you are spending more time thinking it's the right decision to return to work, than thinking it's not, then maybe it's a "good enough" time.

How to make the final decision

Once you have a shortlist of options, it's time to decide. Having too many options is confusing and can paralyze you into indecision.

Exercise 10.5 Decision Making

Step 1. Complete the exercise for each option.

Complete the exercise or take a page of your journal and create a table with 3 columns. Label column 2 "PROS" and column 3 "CONS".

Then in column 1 write:

- How will it affect me?
- How will it affect others?
- Implications and consequences
- Short term effects (less than 1 year)
- Medium term effects (less than 5 years)
- Long term effects (rest of your life)
- Complete the table and then review each option.

Step 2. THEN Make a decision! Take a fresh sheet and write in big letters, your decision.

For example:

"I am going to return to work as secretary" OR

"I am going train to be a lion-tamer"

Julie's decision

If you have been following Julie, you will know that she was trying to decide what direction her career was to take. Exercise 10.5 was a turning point; she realized that while her children were still at home and her husband was employed, working full-time was not a good option. So she planned to find part-time work as a pediatric nurse. She committed to not working more than 25 hours a week. She was concerned that this restriction in hours would be problematic, but when she proposed it to her existing employers, they accepted readily, as it was as she was such a committed, hardworking employee.

How to plan your return to work

Once you have made the decision, it's time to laser focus and be efficient. Complete Exercise 3.1 "Personal Development Plan", for "returning to work", write an action plan and take action. Review your progress regularly. If you need to get a job because you urgently need more money and after two months you haven't had a single interview, you may need to consider going back to the drawing board.

While you are in the process of applying for jobs and hopefully getting interviews, there are some things you should consider doing:

- Get your house in order: Get as organized as you can in all of the other areas of your life. I have failed to this myself to great cost. When you return to work you are not going to have time to sort out your child's bookshelves and sock drawers. Do it while you have time.
- Spend time brushing up on your skills, networking and becoming an expert; make yourself an irresistible employee.

How to get a job

Whether you are returning to work after a long break or looking for a new job, here's a basic guide to get you started:

- Get support from a coach or friend, at the outset.
- Clearly define your desired job or career.
- Research extensively: Potential new job or career, employers, job market and necessary skills or training.
- Apply for jobs: This can be done online through a general or specialized site or you may want to register with a recruitment agency.
- Fill any skill gaps with training or education.
- Networking: See below.
- Write your resume and covering letter, after doing some research. Resume writing has changed considerably in the digital age. Consider getting some help from a friend who is an employer or find help locally and online. Get people to read and edit it for you. Then send it out to employers or agencies. Make it irresistible and interesting.
- Create a business card and keep it simple. Take your cards everywhere you go, you never know when you might meet a potential employer
- Get confident: See Chapter 7.
- Before any interview, practice interview technique. It is essential that you research the company and plan some questions to ask them. Go back to the job description: What might they ask you? Be prepared for questions such as "why are you changing job", "why have you been out of work" and "how you will cope with the job, being a mom".
- Choosing the job. If you are extremely lucky, you may get offered more than one job. If you are struggling to decide which one to take, repeat the exercises 10.4 The Right Job and 10.5 Decision Making.
- Negotiate if needed regarding hours, flexibility, money and benefits. Be confident but not too pushy.
- Make your choice.
- Then, make the best of it. No regrets. Once you have accepted the job, focus on making the job work for you.

Networking

Networking is essential whether you are thinking about returning to work, looking for a new job, established in a job or running a business. It involves connecting with a group of individuals with a common interest or goal. Choose a group of individuals you aspire to be like. Networking can be very valuable for several reasons: Research, finding out about training, finding jobs and getting your confidence back. The networking mindset is important: See it as an opportunity to share your story and talents with people, who may one day, NEED what you do. Options:

- Get out your address book and contact old colleagues.
- Join a local networking group. Take plenty of business cards and hand them out, join conversations and collect other people's cards. Always dress and behave as if you are about to meet the person, who is will change your life. When you get home, promptly, contact the people you met, just to say hello, then contact them again, if and when appropriate.
- Join virtual networking groups including LinkedIn (www.linkedin. com). Then join sub-groups in your field of interest and post or join discussions. It's a great way to network in your pajamas. If you are starting up a business, LinkedIn activity is an excellent way to increase your online visibility. Other social media sites such as Facebook, Twitter and Google+ are also useful, but ever changing.
- Get yourself out there: You never know who you might meet at informal networks such as school events, religious groups, sporting events and even dinner with friends. I have met future clients at a soccer game, in a coffee shop and a visit to my physical therapist, while doing ab-crunches.

A couple of years ago, I went to a networking event on a dark, cold December night. I really didn't want to go but donned my best dress, styled my hair and tried to get in the mood. As I trudged through the snow in my high heels, I thought "what am I doing here?" I went in, turned on the smile, and when the presenter, a New York radio-show host asked for volunteers, to tell their story, I stood up and told mine. My story was featured on the radio the following morning. Months later, the host recorded an interview with me, which appeared on the show five days running. So glad I didn't stay home to watch TV!

A word of caution about networking: You need to be selective as you only have a finite amount of time and energy. Be clear that the group can add value to your situation. If you don't get anything concrete from a meeting be sure to congratulate yourself on making the effort to attend, many people don't bother. Networking rarely yields instant benefits, but if you network consistently, people will get to know you and one day, your big break may come.

How to make working, work

So once you have a job, no matter the what, where, why, how and with whom; the fact remains you are still going to be a mom, and you still deserve to be happy, healthy and successful. Getting the balance right can be hard, however. There will be times when you need to be in two places at once: When you have to choose between family and work. And there will be times when you feel overwhelmed and question your decision. All of these problems are completely normal and commonplace. If and when, these problems arise: Notice them, forgive yourself, safe in the knowledge that you are not the only mom who has ever felt this way.

Time management is hugely important to staying sane, as a working mom. The women who do best as working moms are super-organized. Don't worry if this doesn't describe you right now, if you work hard you CAN improve your organizational skills (see Chapter 5).

The challenges of being a working mom include:

- How to keep the job (hint: Become an invaluable employee)
- How to enjoying the job (managing stress is the key)
- Finding quality time with your children, partner, family and friends.
- Keeping your home from disappearing under a pile of dirty laundry, unopened mail and dust.
- Earning and saving enough money to make it financially viable.
- Finding time to meet your own needs.

Returning to work or moving to a more challenging role, can be a big shock to the system. The work may be harder or more stressful; you may not be able to relate to your colleagues, especially the young, carefree ones; you may find the commute more tiring than you expected and you may end up with the boss from Hell. Expect the unexpected and keep an open mind. Try and notice "what went well" and learn from what went badly.

How to be a happy, healthy successful stay-at-home mom

Being a stay-at-home mom deserves more societal recognition: It can be a tough job.

Whether you are a mom who actively chooses to stay at home or can't return to work because it is not feasible: You deserve to be happy, healthy and successful.

Your level of perceived satisfaction with your role as stay-at-home mom will affect your feelings of wellbeing. If you are a stay-at-home mom who loves being at home, cherishes every moment with your children, does household chores with a smile on your face and a spring in your step and feels great pride in your accomplishments: Then you will flourish. Sadly many moms do not feel this way: They feel bored, frustrated, unhappy, neglected and under-appreciated. If this describes you and returning to work is not an option, you owe it to yourself and your family to change the way you feel. You will be a better parent, wife and role model, for your child if you can increase your level of satisfaction with your role.

The place to start is with accepting that you deserve to be happy, healthy and successful: That you deserve to have your needs met at a high level.

Exercise 10.5 My life as a Stay at Home Mom
Answer the following questions:

- How would I rate my life satisfaction today? (0 = totally dissatisfied, 10 = totally satisfied)
- How would I rate my life satisfaction in the last 3 months?
- What level of life satisfaction do I deserve and desire?
- What are the good points of being a stay at home mom?
- What are the bad points of being a stay at home mom?

- What would I change if I could?
- What do I desire more of?
- What do I desire less of?
- What do I desire to feel, more often?
- What do I desire to feel, less often?
- I feel passionate when…
- I feel energetic when…
- I feel positive when…
- I feel certain when…
- I feel significant when…
- I feel loved when…
- I feel I am growing, progressing or developing when…
- I feel I am contributing when…

If you are feeling dissatisfied, with your life as a stay-at-home mom, complete exercise 3.1 "Personal Development Plan". Focus action on increasing your levels of passion, energy, positivity, certainty, significance, love, growth and contribution. THEN take action. Go on, you deserve it!

Mary's career

Mary was a stay at home mom and parent of a ten year old son with epilepsy and learning difficulties, when she came for coaching. She was deeply unhappy, feeling depressed, lonely, under-employed and lost. Her pre-child career was as an office manager. Mary was considering starting her own business. Working through many of the exercises in this book, Mary came to the conclusion that the time was not right for her to set up a business; her son's needs were too demanding of her time and energy. We talked at length about her situation; I helped her see that her current role was incredibly valuable and that she could be happy as a stay-at-home mom. In order to meet her need for growth, she took an online social media course, for when she was ready to return to work and volunteered as a fundraiser, for an epilepsy charity.

Chapter 10 Summary

- Being a mom is a challenging career.
- The right career, job or role can help you flourish: To be happy, healthy and successful. Flourishing moms create flourishing families.
- The decision to work is a complex and personal one.
- There are many pros and cons to being a working mom.
- Moms who are unhappy with their current career, job or role should give thought to changing their career.

This chapter has guided you through several stages, to help you make an excellent decision about your career change:

- Career audit
- Career development plan
- Consideration of the pros and cons of working
- How to decide what job to do
- Making the decision to change career
- Planning the return to work
- How to get a job
- How to make working, work.

Lastly this chapter offered a way to improve satisfaction with the role of stay-at-home mom.

Chapter 11

 **FINANCES**

any women have misconceptions about money. So let's start this chapter with some truths about money.

Money facts:

- Financial wealth can improve your quality of life and that of your family members.
- Money and wealth are not vulgar.
- The scared ostrich approach to money is not okay.
- Women deserve to be financially successful.
- You are very likely to live beyond retirement age, so you need to have a financial plan for yourself beyond that.
- Your time, skills, education and experience are all just as valuable as that of a man.
- Money can help you provide for yourself, your household, your children, your parents and the community.
- You CAN get proficient at managing your money.

- Many "rich" people are extremely generous, ethical, compassionate people.
- Dealing with your finances is NOT your partner's job: It is a shared responsibility.

I have a confession. I am one of those women who have had a dysfunctional relationship with money. Writing this chapter is as much for me as it is for you!

Sadly, many women neglect their finances. Remember Exercise 2.2 "The Wheel of Life?" Failing to manage your money will make your wheel asymmetrical and your ride very bumpy.

I have met so many women who are complacent about their finance situation. They go through life assuming everything will be okay, especially if they are married: After all their partner will look after them, right?

Here are three cautionary tales to help you take your financial situation seriously.

Helen's Financial Crisis

Helen was a 61 year old woman when she came for coaching. She had been married to a successful engineer; they had 2 kids and had travelled the world with his job. They led an extravagant expat lifestyle; their kids went to private school and life was good. Shortly after his retirement, her partner died suddenly, after a lifetime of working too hard and overindulgence. Struggling to cope with the sudden loss of her partner, Helen was faced with more bad news. It turned out that her partner had minimal life insurance; his pension was paid to him alone and expired on his death; he had recently remortgaged their house to buy a boat and he left behind massive credit card debts. At the age of 60 Helen faced financial disaster. Forced to sell her home and rent a much smaller house and take a job as a homecare assistant to make ends meet. If only she had thought to sit down with her partner and learn about her financial situation. Her partner was a good man but had been complacent about planning for her; if they had only had a conversation, I'm sure he would have provided for her better.

Irene's Financial Crisis

Irene was a 42 when I first started coaching her. She had been married to her childhood sweetheart for 20 years; they had one son and had a great life, full of travel and luxury. Then one day she accidently opened his bank statement. She had never known how much her partner earned; he gave her a very generous allowance every month and she never wanted for anything. She couldn't help but look through the statement and noticed several large regular payments, which turned out to be rent, allowance and school fees for his mistress and daughter. She felt like the bottom fell out of her world. A quick divorce followed. So that things would be settled quickly, she accepted money to buy a new, much smaller house and a modest alimony. However, she found that she could barely live on the allowance, never mind pay for school trips etcetera for their 15 year old son. So at the age of 42 she found herself with no savings, no retirement plan, a small life insurance policy, no college or university savings for her son (who wanted nothing to do with his father) and to top it all she had not worked for over 20 years. She never needed to, before now.

Cynthia's Financial Crisis

Cynthia was a single mom of a 10 year old girl, with severe autism. She worked for a large corporation, who were very supportive of her family situation. Her separation from her daughter's father was traumatic and violent. She did not claim alimony from her ex, as she wanted a clean sheet. Sensibly she maxed out on her pension payments and had good health insurance, but minimal savings. When her daughter developed seizures at the age of 8, things began to fall apart. Several days each month her daughter was too sick to go to school, and her babysitter quit, unable to deal with a sick child. Eventually, Cynthia found a local lady, who had been a nurse, to care for her daughter, when she was not able to go to school. The problem was that the childcare costs were spiraling. It took 12 months for Cynthia's daughter's education plan to be altered so that she could board at a specialist school. By the end of this time, Cynthia was almost wiped out financially.

Now these are extreme stories, but it's time to ask yourself: "Am I financially secure enough to weather all the possible worst case scenarios? Anywhere near? If not, it's time to take urgent action.

Possible worst case scenarios

Now you should know by now, I am not into negative thinking or excessive worry; but the reality is you might face one of these situations, and you need to ask yourself "I am financially ready?" Possible worst case scenarios:

- You get sick.
- You lose your job.
- Family member gets sick and needs expensive care.
- Your partner leaves you or dies.
- Your partner gets sick or loses his job.
- There is a major recession.
- A big unexpected expense (home repairs, new car etc).
- A financial institution you have invested in goes bankrupt, and you lose your assets.
- A loved one needs a financial bail-out.

Financial Knowledge is Power

According to Richard Kiyosaki, *"it is not money, but knowledge that makes you rich"*. So how much do you know about your financial situation, in real, accurate, up to the minute terms? The financial world is all about numbers. The more you know; the more power you have to alter your situation.

This next exercise is designed to give you an accurate picture of your financial situation, and it may require some research. You may need to gather some of this information from your partner, your bank or your broker. Tell them that you are sorting out your finances and want to get up to date information. With your partner, you need to be tactful and cautious: This is not meant to be a snooping or threatening exercise, at all. Ultimately YOU are the only one who has a 100% vested interest in YOUR financial situation.

Exercise 11.1 Finance Audit

Step 1. Complete the exercise or record:

- Income: How much money do you have coming in? From job income or business profit to bank interest or dividends on shares.

What is your total family income?

- Expenses: Money flowing out of your possession. These include grocery bills, mortgage payments, telephone bills and taxes.

- Assets: Financially valuable resources that you own or control. Basically, anything that you could sell to generate cash. They can be tangible, such as a car; or intangible such as shares. An asset can only be counted as an asset if there is equity tied to it and there is little chance of the value decreasing significantly.

Asset = cash value – liability

Examples:

Home asset = current market value – mortgage – cost to sell

Stock asset = current market value (varies daily) – cost to sell

- Liabilities: Financial obligations. For example: Credit card debt; a property with a mortgage or expenses to keep your car at its' current market value (servicing etc).

- Retirement savings.

- Insurance policies. You should know the monthly payments, level of protection, terms
    - ◊ Life
    - ◊ Illness
    - ◊ Redundancy
    - ◊ Health
    - ◊ Travel
    - ◊ Car
    - ◊ Home
    - ◊ Umbrella
    - ◊ Other

Step 2. Once you have collected and analyzed the data. Answer the following question: What do you think of your financial situation NOW?

Step 3. Complete Exercise 3.1 "Personal Development Plan" for "Financial Situation", if you are concerned about your financial situation.

Step 4. Then create an action plan for the next 3 months and then TAKE ACTION.

Step 5. Review your progress at regular intervals, revisit your data and make a new action plan if needed.

5 steps to improving your finances

Step 1. Increase income

Step 2. Budget

Step 3. Protect your money

Step 4. Increase your financial knowledge

Step 5. Change your mindset

Step 1: Increase income

According to the American International Revenue Service in the USA there are three broad types of income:

1. **Active or earned income:**
   - Someone in the family gets a job
   - Work more hours
   - Get a higher paid job
   - Set up a business

2. **Passive income**

   Passive income is regular income, earned with little ongoing effort. There is usually, however, some effort required at the set-up phase. Examples include interest on savings, royalties on a book or song and rental income. Benefits from the government, such as social security benefits (in USA) and unemployment benefit (in UK), might also be considered passive income.

3. **Portfolio income**

   These are the profits made from selling an investment, such as shares or property. An initial investment of time and money is needed, prior to purchasing the investment. Investments vary enormously in their risk and return.

Budget

Budgeting is the discipline of planning your spending. The aim is to determine in advance if you will have enough money, to cover your expenses and your liabilities, and perhaps to save or invest.

Step 1. Collect data on income and current spending on a balance sheet.

Step 2. Determine if you have a surplus of money (money left over) or a deficit (not enough money).

Step 3. Plan either what to spend your money on or how to cover the deficit.

If don't already or haven't ever kept a family balance sheet, I would recommend you do the next exercise.

Exercise 11.2 Balance Sheet

Go back two to five months and collect as much data on income and spending as you can. Then for the next month keep accurate records. Keep all receipts and cross reference them against bank statements. Categorize your income and spending and calculate category totals for each month.

Income categories:
- Active
- Passive
- Portfolio

Spending categories:
- Auto and transport
- Bills and utilities
- Cash
- Children: Necessities
- Children: Non-necessities
- Deposit to savings

- Eating out
- Education
- Entertainment
- Fees and charges
- Financial
- Fitness
- Gifts and donations
- Health
- Home: General
- Home: Mortgage interest
- Home: Mortgage payments
- Home: Rent
- Pets
- Shopping: Groceries and household
- Shopping: Other
- Tax
- Travel
- Other: Your own categories or subcategories.

Then calculate:

Monthly total income – total expenses = surplus or deficit

Get in the habit of collecting data to complete your balance sheet every month. It is a great way to focus attention on spending, and usually reduces it.

There are some excellent personal finance software programs and apps (such as Quicken), if you are a technophile.

Surplus

If you find you have a surplus, you need to plan, what to do with it? Your many choices include: Letting it sit in a low interest account (just in case you need it), spending it, investing it or purchasing a new asset. Consider your priorities. What are you going to do with any surplus, this month and in the future?

Deficit

If you have a deficit then how will you reduce it? Ideas include: Earn more money, move money from assets or savings, or borrow money. If you borrow choose a low risk, low interest source.

If your deficit is part of a larger debt, you need to take action.

According to Richard Kiyosaki, in his book Unfair Advantage, there are two types of debt:

1. Good debt: This debt is purposeful, you can afford to pay it off comfortably and you are getting a good deal on the loan. An example of good debt: Mortgage on a buy-to-let property that makes you a good profit, and has a low mortgage rate.
2. Bad debt: Includes unplanned debt, debt that is beyond your means to pay off or expensive debt, such as credit card debt.

Being in "bad" debt can create stress, and we all know that stress is bad for your health, wellbeing, performance and relationships.

I am not going to go any further into talking about debt, but if this is concern, I urge you to seek advice from a reputable organization or advisor.

Preventing future deficits

If you find that you are in debt or frequently have a monthly deficit, you are going to need to look closely at increasing your income, reducing spending or better protecting your income.

There are many ways to reduce spending such as cutting up your credit cards; looking for good deals on items you must buy; avoiding buying in haste and setting a monthly budget, then sticking to it. To avoid buying in haste try this: If you see something you like, write it down and review in 48 hours. Do you still want it, or could you live without it?

Step 2: Budget

Next it's time for budgeting. Use your results from Exercise 11.2, to help you budget, for each category of spending, for the months ahead. For example, you may calculate your "personal care" budget and realize that you can only achieve this by getting a hair cut every eight weeks, instead of six, or shaving your legs instead of paying for waxing. Then monitor your spending at least weekly. If you find you are spending too much on one area, then you need to find ways to cut back, or review the budget. For example: If you find you are spending too much on food, but are being very careful, then your budget was unrealistic and needs to be increased. But, if you find that two weeks into the month you have spent your "eating out" budget, then you may need to decide not to eat out again this month.

This process takes discipline and practice, but you will be amazed at how it focuses your attention and how much money you will save.

Step 3: Protect your money

The next step is protecting your money and your assets.

There are many ways you can fail to protect your money and end up with less money in your pocket. Here are a few and how to reduce the risk:

Taxes

Paying taxes is one of the responsibilities of citizens, living in a fair society. With taxes the people who govern us can provide education, healthcare, emergency services, defence, welfare and so on. But many people are paying more on tax then they need to be. Getting good tax advice can save you money.

Banks

Banks are essential institutions for saving and borrowing money. As we have learned in recent years, most banks do not have the customer's best interests in mind and are looking to make money from you and your money. Shopping around and researching to find: The lowest bank charges for your debt, the highest interest rates for your savings and the best terms and conditions for your accounts, will save you money and is well worth the time and effort.

Financial salespeople

These include stock brokers and insurance brokers. Again do your homework and don't forget they may not have your best interest in mind. Be financially knowledgeable and keep in mind that it's your hard earned money and bargain for the best deal.

Financial predators

It's unsettling to think that there are people in the world wanting to take your money without your permission; there have always been such people, but now they are more sophisticated and have access to the internet. Here are some simple tips on how to protect yourself:

- If it's too good to be true, it is probably not true.
- Never give out personal information without being SURE who you are giving it too. Ask them to give you their information and call them back, when you have checked. Tell bank staff that you'd rather come into the branch.
- Your friend who is stranded is the Philippines having been robbed and urgently needing your help is probably tucked up at home in her bed, and you have not won a lottery you did not enter.

Insurance

Insurance is a way of protecting your life against adverse effects. Essential insurance policies include life insurance, home insurance and car insurance. Health insurance is essential in countries without socialized medicine. You may also want to consider long-term care insurance, redundancy insurance, ill-health insurance etc. It is essential to shop around, to read the small print and look out for exclusions or co-pays.

Step 4: Get a financial education

Isn't it amazing that most of us spent at least 12 years in formal education, but learned nothing about how to manage our own money? I am one of those! I left University after 18 years of education not knowing how to budget, balance my accounts or invest my money. For me writing this book gave me the incentive to learn more: I hope it will do the same for you. Read reputable books, taking a course, join an investment club, read financial magazines or newspapers (at your level of understanding). There is a lot of information out there; so much, that it's rather overwhelming. Be very picky about who chose to learn from. Beware of opinions; seek out facts. Keep as much control of your money as you can and remember the idea is to make your money work for you, to meet your needs. High risk investing may be okay for an adrenaline junkie who has lots of spare cash, but for a cautious person with little financial safety net, this approach is likely to make you nervous and uncertain.

Step 5: Change your mindset

Why do so many women have a weird mindset when it comes to money? Here are some of the unhelpful money mindsets that I encounter a lot with women:

- Money doesn't make people happy.
- Money is the root of evil.
- Women can never earn as much as men.
- I'm a mom; I can't waste money on me.
- I will never be rich, so why bother trying.
- It's better to do voluntary work than earn money.
- I don't deserve to buy nice things for myself.
- I'll be okay; I can always live off welfare.
- My partner will take care of me.
- I don't trust anyone with my money.
- My savings will be safe in the bank.
- My partner deals with all of the financial stuff.
- I should offer my product and services to my friends for free.
- It's only money.

If you hold any of these beliefs, it's time to work on your financial mindset.

Taking responsibility

I urge you to take 100% responsibility for your finances. What do I mean by this? Well, take responsibility for the aspects of your financial situation, you can affect. I don't mean you need to earn 100% of your family's income or control all of your family's spending; this is just not possible or desirable for many women. But here are some examples. For example: If you are working and fail to ask for a raise when you know you deserve it; you are not taking 100% responsibility. If you know your savings are sitting in an account with a terrible interest rate but you can't be bothered to move it to a better account; you are not taking 100% responsibility. If your children's spending or your partner's spending is out of control and you do nothing; you are not taking 100% responsibility.

Money is not vulgar, evil, dangerous or harmful. Money in the hands of someone with poor values and low integrity can be all of these. Money in the hands of a person with good values and high integrity can be powerful force for good.

The next exercise will start you on the path to changing your money mindset.

Exercise 11.3 The Money Mantra

Stand up and put your hand on your heart. Say out loud the following sentences with conviction.

- I deserve to be wealthy and financially secure
- I am responsible for my own financial situation
- Increasing my wealth, will increase my wellbeing
- With increased wealth, I can do more good in the world

How did you feel?

Did you feel uncomfortable or like a fraud saying any of these sentences?

Think back to Chapter 2, when you connected with your "authentic self" and in particular your values system and needs profile.

Exercise 11.4 Values, needs and money

Complete the exercise or draw a table with 2 columns.

In column 1: Write down your top five values and your top five needs.

In column 2: Write down any ways that having more money would let you live up to your value system and meet your needs.

Repeat your money mantra. Do you feel more congruent repeating is now?

Julie's Finances

Julie had some self limiting beliefs about wealth. She had grown up believing that rich people were dishonest, and that money would always be scarce. In the mantra, the line: "I deserve to be wealthy and financially secure" was very difficult for her to say confidently. Exercise 11.4 helped Julie change her mindset and realise that not only did she deserve to be wealthy, but money was essential to helping her and her family create the life she desired. Here are some of her responses:

"Value: Love. Having more money could allow me to do more fun things with my family, let me work less hours and have more quality time with my family. I could afford to travel to see my family and friends and connect with them more.

"Value: Health. Having more money could allow me to buy better quality food, take cooking lessons, join a gym, see the best doctor when I am sick, get help with managing my stress, stop smoking.

Need: Certainty. Having more money would increase my certainty that Max and I would be able to retire comfortably, that my kids would be provided for if I die, that we can afford to go on vacation, that we can keep the roof over our heads.

Need: Significance. With more money, I can give to charity, buy clothes that make me feel good, get a really good haircut and host a party for my friends."

Crooked thinking

Chapter 7's section on "crooked thinking" should be revisited if you have remaining mindset barriers regarding money.

Charity

Giving to charity is a wonderful way to contribute to the community and can make you feel good about yourself. However, according to Suze Orman in Women and Money, we need to be sure we are giving money or our time (which equates to lost earnings) for the right reasons. Here are six questions you should ask yourself when we are giving either time or money:

1. Is my intent towards the receiver positive?
2. Am I being true to my authentic self?
3. Am I giving to say "thank you" or "I love you" or "I would like to offer this freely to you" OR to get something back? If it's the latter, you may resent giving, if they don't reciprocate.
4. Is giving this going to affect me adversely? Only give what you can really afford to give.
5. Is this gift of time or money going to be a burden to the receiver? Don't give if the other person does not want to receive; it will not make them happy or may make them feel disempowered or indebted to you.
6. Is it the right time for me to give and the receiver to receive?

Money and the two partner household

The financial contribution of partners, to the family income varies enormously. As does the spending patterns, in families. In some families, one partner pays for everything, in some it is split 50-50 and in others there are all sorts of complex arrangements: Like dad pays for the mortgage and healthcare; mum pays for groceries and clothes. There is no right or wrong, but mutual agreement is essential.

Money disputes in families are often about more than just money. Things that can complicate financial issues include: partners not getting along; one partner feeling like their needs are not being met; other family members making demands; parenting conflicts or one partner being intensely unhappy at work. Dialogue and transparency over money can prevent this. When you have worked out your family balance sheet for a few months, you are in a really good position to sit down and talk about money: With facts to discuss. Tell your partner that you'd like to have a chat about money, so that you can agree on how to improve your family's financial situation. Make sure you are non-threatening but clear on your goals for the "chat". You discuss whether to buy more assets, budget or reduce debt. Tell your partner you really appreciate how hard they work, and you want to make sure you are doing everything you can, to ensure a comfortable financial future for your family.

Two parent household, where you are a stay-at-home mom

I have met many stay-at-home moms who do not spend much money on themselves, even if their family can afford it. I think this has something to do with the guilt of not earning, gratitude to their partner for letting them stay home and feeling like their kids or partner deserve nicer things than them. I had a client who did not buy herself new glasses for five years, despite the prescription now being way too weak; yet she would spend $80 on a skirt for her daughter, for one party, when her daughter already had a wardrobe full of clothes. There are of course moms at the other end of the spectrum, who spend more money on themselves, than their family budget can afford. Overspending can be part of a larger problem such as depression, shopping addiction, boredom and compulsive behaviors.

The job of being a stay-at-home mom usually doesn't involve a paycheck; consequently some moms find it hard to value themselves. If this is you, STOP, right now! Being a stay-at-home mom is an extremely valuable job. Just think what it would cost if you had to outsource all of the things you do for your family. Make an estimate of how many hours you work for your family, each week. Work includes: Childcare, washing, cleaning, ironing, attending meetings at school, walking the dog and going to the post office. Multiply the hours by the minimum wage or what you would pay for a cleaner or babysitter in your town. How much do you come up with: A sizeable amount of money, right? And don't forget you are THE EXPERT on what your family wants and needs. Imagine what you'd pay an expert to do all of those jobs.

For many moms, myself included (big time), coming to terms with not contributing to the family income, can be difficult and uncomfortable. It can be quite an adjustment to see your partner's income as FAMILY income. One way to ease this transition is to stay actively involved in your family's finances. For example, you may want to create and monitor the family budget or take on paying the bills. The extent of involvement is up to you. Whatever your situation, it is in the best interest of your family, that there is transparency about finances and frequent dialogue. No-one likes a financial surprise. The more often you have these conversations; the easier they become. If there is not enough money coming into the household to meet even the most basic bills, you must make a plan to address this; this is not a sustainable situation.

If your family has a surplus, then you need to come up with the best way for your family to invest, spend or save.

Two parent household where you are the main breadwinner

This is an increasingly common situation. It can work well, but may cause tension. Traditionally men gain significance by being the main provider for the family, making it a hard role to give up, although I know several men who would love it! You will need to put some effort into helping your partner meet his need for significance, personally or by encouraging him to find other avenues, such as playing his favorite sport or time to pursue a hobby. Transparency and frequent dialogue will help prevent tension over this perceived imbalance.

Money and the single mom

When you are a single mom, most of the decisions about money are down to you, and this can seem overwhelming. Some single moms receive financial support from their ex; others don't. There is no denying it; being a single mom can be hard. Your ability to earn will depend on many factors including your support networks, potential income and your child or children. If you add into the equation a sick or special needs child, then earning enough to support the family can be even more challenging.

There are many single moms who use their single-mom-ness to drive them to work harder, smarter or in a more inventive way. With the rise of jobs like "virtual assistant", if you have skills and motivation you can earn money no matter what your situation. If you don't have skills: Go and get them. You owe it to yourself and your child to grow and optimize your financial situation.

Money and children

Things haven't changed all that much since you and I were kids, with regards to teaching personal finance to children. Imagine that your child at 18, knew what you know now; if they could avoid the financial mistakes that you have made and they could be wealthy, wise, kind and compassionate with money. Wouldn't that be great? Well they can; but you might have to guide them.

Teach your child what you have learned in this book and seek out other reliable sources of information: Games, courses, videos and clubs. Your child is their future. Teach them well and it will be a great one.

Don't be afraid of sharing some details of your financial situation with your child. There's no need to tell them the family income or how much debt you are in, but dishonesty with your child shows them no respect. If you are in debt and are not sure how you will manage, tell your child calmly. Explain you need to tighten your belts, and you really need their help doing this. You will be amazed at how insightful children can be, if you are honest with them.

If your family is well off and there is no scarcity of money, you need to work hard to help your children respect money and have a good attitude towards money and hard work. In Darren Hardy's book, "*The Compound Effect*", he states that wealth often skips a generation. This fact is probably because children of wealthy parents have had life too easy, and they don't value money and hard work, as much as poorer kids. Of course, this is a generalization but worth avoiding if you can.

I recommend from the age of about 10, giving your child a small allowance. Allow them to earn extra money by doing additional chores. Set out your ground rules for spending. For example, your child buys luxury items such as video games, junk food, trips to the movies and maybe even clothes, with their allowance. No bail outs, no advancements, no excuses. They will learn that if they want something non-essential, they will have work for it or at least wait until they have saved up for it, or receive birthday money. When I did this for my boys, one spent his first week's allowance on slushies; he was genuinely shocked that the money was all gone. The next week: No slushies!

Sandra's dilemma

Sandra asked me for advice about her her eldest child, who had gone to College. She generously gave him a credit card to be used only for rent, food and education supplies, like books. She agreed to pay for the bill, for these essentials. She started to notice an increasing trend for spending on coffee, lunches out and a lot of spending on books. Turned out he was buying books for poorer friends with the promise that they would pay him back later. When she asked me what to do I explained that I thought it was good for young people to experience some scarcity of money and that she needed to be very honest with him, he was 19 after all. I told her that if she really loved him she needed to teach him about money. Just like never teaching your child to cook or tidy up, not teaching them to manage money does them no favors in the long term. So she came up with a plan.

Next time her son was home, she sat him down and was honest with him. She told him she was proud of the man he had become, but she felt bad that she had not taught him how to manage money. She showed him how to budget, clarified the rules for the credit card and showed him some useful online tools for managing money. The meeting went well; he felt that he was being respected and understood that he needed to take more responsibility. It is a conversation that he will probably never forget.

Your financial situation can be a source of great stress or of confident certainty. If you have remaining concerns regarding your financial situation, return to Chapter 3 and complete Exercise 3.1 "Personal Development Plan" for "financial situation" or "money".

Chapter 11 Summary

You deserve to have a healthy relationship with money. Money can be a great source for good, in the right hands. It can help you live a happy, healthy, successful life.

You need to be prepared for worst-case scenarios like your partner leaving you or losing your job.

Financial power comes from financial knowledge and responsibility.

In order to improve your financial situation, you first need a clear picture of your current situation.

Next, make a plan to improve your financial situation. Steps might include:

Step 1. Increasing income

Step 2. Budgeting and reducing spending.

Step 3. Protecting your money.

Step 4. Increasing your financial knowledge.

Step 5. Changing your mindset.

Families all have unique financial situations, which require unique solutions.

Begin your child's financial education early; they will thank you for it one day.

Chapter 12

ENVIRONMENT

*Y*our environment is everything outside of you. There are two main aspects to your environment, which we will consider in this chapter: Your physical environment and your situation.

Your physical environment includes your planet, country, region, town or city, street, neighborhood and home. Your situation ranges from your marital status, the number of children you have, having a child with additional needs, any recent bereavements, through to your employment status.

Your environment greatly influences how you experience your world; it is however, a part of your life over which you may have little influence. Where you do have influence, you have the power to create the environment you choose. For example: If you dislike the decoration in your home, redecorate or add finishing touches; if you worry about global warming, become vegetarian. When you do not have influence, you can still change our perspective and therefore, the effect it has on you. For example: If you have moved house and are struggling to settle into your new town, you could focus on building a positive social network around you and spending time meditating, to reduce stress.

Physical Environment

Your planet

You live on an amazing planet, which supports the human race and the estimated 7.7 million species of animals, and 298,000 species of plants. Our planet sits in a solar system, which resides within the vast expanse of the Universe.

There is increasing concern about the impact human activity is having on our planet. My personal view, and it is just my perspective, is that we need to give urgent thought to how our behavior affects our environment. Concerns include air pollution caused by factories, meat production and transportation; the use of GM crops and toxic substances in farming; destruction of natural habitats such as rainforest; and contamination of land and drinking water supplies. This damage, in the long term will harm us, our children and generations to come. One day, the damage may reach a critical point where it can no longer reversible, and serious environmental consequences will be inevitable; such as rising sea levels, extinction of species or depletion of the ozone layer.

How to do "your bit for the environment"

There are many thousands of ways you can help our environment and protect your planet for future generations. Here are my top 10 ideas:

1. Treasure, enjoy and respect the environment and teach your children to do the same.
2. Volunteer your time to help an environmental cause.
3. Donate money to environmental charities: Research to find those with a good track record.
4. Consider reducing your meat consumption or becoming vegetarian: The meat industry is a major producer of green-house gases.
5. Get educated on environmental issues by reading, attending talks or joining an environmental newsletter.
6. Buy produce from local organic farmers. This supports local farmers, reduces land and food contamination and reduces pollution from transportation. Did you know much of the salad produced in the USA

is grown in California? This means that if you live in Maine, your salad may have travelled 3,500 miles to get to you; not only is that a lot of fuel consumption but it means that your salad has lost much of its' nutrition by the time it gets to you.

7. Grow trees, flowers and crops. Plants are nature's way of reducing atmospheric carbon dioxide. Composting garden and kitchen waste will produce organic compost for next year's plants.

I'm a total novice gardener, and I am really not into hard labor. While writing this book I had my first season of growing salad, fruit and vegetables, all in containers on my deck. I also grew wheatgrass and sprouting seeds, in my kitchen, to add to salads. My kids helped with composting and with watering and picking the produce, and are amazed by what we have grown. Overall, a great experience.

8. Recycling: There are many things that can be recycled like clothes, plastics, paper and metal. Donating used items to organizations such as thrift shops, community sites such as www.freecycle.com and charities, prevents items going into landfill, puts items to good use and saves valuable resources.

9. Reduce water, electricity and fuel use. Ways to do this include: Unplugging electrical items when not in use, watering lawns sparingly, turning the thermostat down a couple of degrees in winter (there's a great invention called the sweater that can ease the pain of this) and batch errands to reduce car usage.

10. Minimize use of disposable items such as cutlery on a picnic, plastic grocery shopping bags and even diapers. A favorite tip of mine, courtesy of my mother in law, from the 1950s is to use empty cereal bags as sandwich bags for your child's lunch.

Your Country

If you are reading this book it is likely you live in a developed country, with a high standard of living. Yet you may be dissatisfied with your country for a variety of reasons including: Politics, laws, culture, lack of job opportunities, financial problems, bad weather, you don't feel welcome (if you from a minority group or are an immigrant), distance from loved ones and poor healthcare or education.

Expats and immigrants

Expatriates or expats are often living in a foreign country, for a set time period. Immigrants usually remain permanently. It is well documented that expats and immigrants experience difficulties settling into their new country. Common problems are uncertainty, stress and mental health problems. There are many reasons for this and these include:

- Loneliness and separation from loved ones and friends

  It can take several months to establish new friendships. Not speaking the native language, can increase social isolation. Additionally, your new community may not be very welcoming.

  Thankfully, the internet makes it simple to keep in touch with family and friends back home, and this can ease social isolation. Establishing new social connections is important. If you have children of school age, you may find it easier to meet new friends. Some towns have clubs for newcomers or expats and these can be a good source of social connection.

- Cultural differences

  Cultural differences exist between all countries. Some differences you may be able to embrace; others you may dislike. Some differences may be minor such as different food stores; others more significant, such as strange, nonsensical laws. You may have to apply for permission to work in your new country or learn to drive all over again. If you have a professional career you may find that your qualifications are not valid and considerable retraining is necessary, to do your old job. You may find that the way women are valued or treated is different.

  You may struggle with other differences such as the road system, organization of services and availability of your favorite food. Most of the expats yearn for food from home.

  Language differences may cause cultural difficulties. This is most pronounced when a totally different language is spoken, for example if an English speaking person moves to China. There can also be significant geographical or cultural language differences, within a major language. For example, when people relocate from the US to other English speaking countries, they are surprised by the number of differences. One amusing example is the use of the word "pants", which in the USA refers to long trousers and in the UK refers to men's underwear.

When my family moved to the US, from the UK, in 2009, many differences surprised us. For example, it took me six weeks to discover that outgoing mail went into our mailbox, I found the road signage very confusing and I missed meeting friends at the school gate, as my kids now used the school bus system. I had to take a driving course and test, despite driving for 20 years; and was unable to work as a physician. I was fascinated by the language differences. It took me several months to figure out that cilantro meant "coriander" and arugula meant "rocket". One child, I was coaching, corrected me when I said "good boy" and told me in the US, that is what you would say to a dog. My son missed canned Heinz Spaghetti, which he ate nearly every day (as popular in the UK as Mac and Cheese), so a friend once brought, 36 cans in a suitcase. He got through customs with a rather puzzled look from the officer!

- Cost of living

    The cost of living varies greatly around the world. You may move somewhere with higher salaries only to find, that the cost of living is much higher too. Costs include food, fuel, utilities, healthcare, services and taxes. I was horrified when we received our first bill for heating oil. We moved from the UK where we had piped gas, to a town that relied on individual oil supplies. I called the oil company to tell them they had made a terrible mistake. It turned out that it was me, who had made the mistake, oil is very expensive.

- Sorting out finances

    When you move to a new country, your bank history begins from scratch, many banks will decline your custom, and it can be challenging to get credit. This can lead to difficulties with accommodation, buying expensive items such as a car or contract items such as a phone.

- Relationship problems

  Moving to a new country is a major source of stress, and can have a serious impact on relationships; both with the people you have left behind and the family live with. Children can find adapting to a new country challenging and may need additional support. Your relationship with your partner may be put under strain, as it is likely you will adapt to the move differently.

- Healthcare

  Healthcare systems vary country to country, and this change can be hard to adapt to. Also, your new country may have an increased risk of illness you are not accustomed to, like malaria and dysentery in Africa and skin cancer in the Middle East.

- Education

  Your child's education is important, and it can be difficult to find the right school. The school system will be different, with minor issues such as homework policy or school uniform, through to major issues such as examinations offered. Careful thought should be given to moving older children, for whom a change in exam system may be very disruptive.

  The key to minimizing the effects of being an expat or immigrant lie in researching before a move, good planning, actively building social support, making efforts to fit in culturally and stress management (see chapter 7).

- Locality

  You may experience problems due to the region, county, town, neighborhood or street, you live in. Local problems include: Poor air quality, access to healthy food, safety, employment opportunities, education, noisy neighbors, environmental noise, access to open spaces for your child, poor facilities, unreliable utilities, distance from amenities and an unfamiliar local culture.

- Your home

  Your satisfaction with your home will impact your overall satisfaction with life. There are many reasons you may love or hate your home: From locality, size, age, architecture, layout, state of repair, decoration, smell, temperature, outside space, through to tidiness and cleanliness.

If you are unhappy with your physical environment, you owe it to yourself and your family to do something about it. Complete Exercise 3.1 "Personal Development Plan" for "physical environment" or "home".

Sophie's environment

Sophie came to see me, one January morning, months after relocation, due to her husband, Bill's work. They moved from a Sydney, Australia to a sleepy town in Connecticut, USA. They bought their new home after a quick Spring-time visit to the town, three months before the move. They chose the town for its' good schools and ease of travel to her husband's work. The house was double the size of their last and was on a wooded three acre plot, a big change from their third of an acre lawn yard in Sydney. Sophie hated the house from the day they arrived in August, three weeks before her two daughters started school. They arrived in the middle of a heat wave, only to find the house had no central air. The drive to town was much longer than expected and there was not the feel of neighborhood she was used to. Her girls were initially slow to settling into their new school, as friendship circles were well established, but they soon began make new friends. Bill seemed to be unaffected by the move, he knew many of his work-mates already, and his commute to work was shorter than ever before. Bill and Sophie had agreed that she would take a break to settle in before considering work.

Sophie met some moms at school events but didn't really relate to any of them. As winter set in, Sophie became increasingly miserable, she hated the decoration in her home, the harsh winter weather took her by surprise, and her social isolation grew. Sophie shared her thoughts with Bill, and asked that he consider moving the family back to Australia. He replied that he thought she was crazy; they had a stunning home in a lovely town, the girls were settling in and he was doing just fine. Our coaching sessions focused on what Sophie could change reasonably. Together we established her priorities of developing new friendships, designing her home, getting healthy (she had gained 15lbs since the move) and getting back to work. She redecorated several rooms in her home, joined a neighborhood book club, joined a yoga class and began retraining to return to work. We also worked on her perspective and positive thinking, so that over time she was able to appreciate and focus on the favorable aspects of her new home and locality. She avoided slipping back into the depression she had suffered after her first child. After three months, Sophie was enjoying her new life she was making progress towards returning to work; she had lovely group of friends and had returned to her pre-move weight.

Your situation

Your personal or family situation may be a source of stress or unhappiness for you. According to the APA 2012 Stress Survey, the top causes of stress in adults were: Money, work, the economy, family responsibilities, relationships and family and personal health problems.

These findings concur with the widely used "Social Readjustment Rating Scale", in which the top groups of life events which cause stress are:

- Death of spouse or close family member
- Change in relationship status
- Legal problems
- Personal injury or illness
- Change in employment or business status
- Health problems of a family member
- Pregnancy
- Sexual difficulties
- Loss or gain of a family member from the home
- Change in financial status

As discussed previously in this book, your reaction to such life events depends on your perspective and your resources for managing stress.

Because your situation has the potential to significantly affect your health and wellbeing, and that of your loved ones, any aspects of your situation that cause you distress deserve some careful attention.

Bereavement

The loss of a loved one is devastating. Life appears to be turned upside down, for some time. Kubler-Ross's sentinel work, from the 1960s, describes five stages of grief:

Stage 1. Denial
Stage 2. Anger
Stage 3. Bargaining
Stage 4. Depression
Stage 5. Acceptance

Over 20 years of research, has led George Bonnano to conclude, that there are four main types of paths grieving individuals follow:

- Cope fairly well and become more resilient
- Develop some problems such as depression or post-traumatic stress, later returning to pre-bereavement state
- Develop chronic dysfunction, with prolonged suffering and inability to function
- Initially normal reaction with delayed distress or symptoms months later.

If you have experienced a bereavement and are struggling to cope, seeking help from a bereavement expert, may help you recover more quickly, than you could alone.

Change in relationship status

Any change in marital or relationship status will undoubtedly affect your wellbeing. The effects can be positive or negative, depending on the nature of the change. The level to which your needs are met may change dramatically. After a period of settling, people usually adapt to their new situation. The impact on your children is likely to be considerable; they will need support during this time.

Legal difficulties

Legal difficulties can be a great source of uncertainty, stress and financial cost. Whether the legal issue affects you or a loved one; the impact is likely to be negative. Getting support from family and friends or an impartial professional will help you minimize the effects.

Personal injury or illness

Physical injury or illness and mental health problems significantly affect your wellbeing, in all areas of your life. They may cause stress, lack of energy, difficulty focusing, relationship problems and reduced your ability to function normally. Health problems will sabotage your ability to increase wellbeing in other areas of your life, so should be addressed as a matter of urgency. Chapters 6 and 7 deal these issues in greater detail.

Change in employment or business status

If you work full-time, you spend approximately one third of your waking hours at work. So changes in employment status or the success of your business can be unsettling and stressful. Chapter 10 discussed change in career in greater detail.

Family Health Problems

Most moms worry about the health of their family, especially children. You invest so much time, love, energy and commitment into your children. When they are sick, it is extremely stressful and exhausting. In most families when a child is sick, it is mom, who has to put her other responsibilities on hold. I missed several weeks of work, when my eldest son was sick as a baby; I felt terrible about it, but I had no choice.

Caregivers experience significant levels of stress: Whether they are caring for a sick elderly relative or their special needs, disabled or chronically sick child. Stress arises from uncertainty, fear of the future, additional workload, financial burden, parenting challenges, fatigue, reduced access to stress relievers and lack of time to focus on meeting their own needs. According to research from the Waisman Center, the effects of chronic stress in mothers of children with autism mimic that of combat soldiers.

Pregnancy

Pregnancy and the birth of a child herald major changes in a woman's life. Changes occur in your body, emotions, energy levels, ability to function in various tasks, finances, relationships, perspective on the world, priorities, time, and patience.

Sexual difficulties

Many moms experience sexual difficulties, at some time. They vary from sexual response or desire issues, pain on intercourse, emotional problems, negative beliefs about sex, relationship problems; through to lifestyle (a baby who doesn't sleep is not great for sex drive). And then of course your partner may have sexual problems of his own. It is reassuring to know that most sexual problems are short lived. If you experience such problems, honesty with your partner can help reduce the impact. If sexual problems persist, involve pain, affect your relationship or make you depressed or anxious, make an appointment with your doctor.

Loss or gain of a family member from your home

The dynamic of your family home depends largely on the people within it. So, the loss or gain of a family member will alter the wellbeing of your family. Relationships within a family are highly complex, and the effects of change can be unpredictable. When you are a mom, loss or gain of a family member will also impact your workload considerably. I was astonished by the reduction in housework, when my children were at camp for two weeks.

Moms in particular can be affected when children leave home, to lead an independent life. According to the Mayo Clinic, "empty nest syndrome" is when a parent experiences feelings of sadness and loss, due to their last child leaving home. Factors effecting how you will cope include: your support network; your contact with your child; any uncertainty about your child's wellbeing and your adjustment to your new role. Negative effects include a sense of loss, depression, identity crisis and relationship difficulties. However, for many moms, this life stage offers new opportunities, which can be exciting.

The loss or gain of a pet can be a source of great sadness or joy. Pets are of course also a source of work and financial cost for the family, but the benefits connection with a pet can far outweigh the costs. For children, the loss of a pet, even a goldfish can be upsetting. It may be your child's first experience of losing a living being, they are close to. They may begin to ask many questions about life, death, what happens after death and religion. For parents, the death of a pet, can offer opportunities to discuss your families beliefs on these matters.

Change in financial status

Your family's financial situation is fundamental to the wellbeing of your family. Financial uncertainty is a great source of stress for many families. Your finances affect your ability to meet your family's needs from the basic needs of food, water, shelter and safety to your ability to take vacations and for your child to go to college. Chapter 11 discusses financial status in much greater detail.

Moving forward

Finding yourself in a difficult situation such as those above can be stressful, at the time but there is some good news. In his book Flourish, Selligman points to research showing that stressful events can lead to enormous growth and resilience. Some people who experience highly stressful situations can experience "positive-traumatic stress disorder". He found that certain characteristics increase the chances of a positive outcome:

1. Emotional fitness: Including positive thinking and problem-focused coping strategies
2. Social fitness: Trust and friendship with positive social connections
3. Family fitness: Including relationship skills
4. Spiritual fitness: Including moral, ethical and religious beliefs

The following exercise is aimed to help you begin to move forward, in a positive way following a stressful situation or life event.

Exercise 12.1 Moving forward

Step 1. Complete the following statements:
- My situation or life event…
- Effect this has on my:

◊ Emotional health
◊ Physical health
◊ Finances
◊ Relationships
◊ Career/ work
◊ Time
◊ Children
◊ Partner
◊ Family
◊ Friends
◊ Other relationships
◊ Physical environment
◊ Level of certainty
◊ Level of variety, interest and excitement
◊ Level of feeling significant, important, unique, needed
◊ Level of love
◊ Level of connection
◊ Level of growth
◊ Level at which I contribute to others

Now, list any positive effects of this situation or live events (think hard)…

Step 2. Stand up, put your hand on your heart and say out loud: "I deserve to be happy, healthy and successful"

Step 3. Complete the following statements.

• Things I can change about my situation…
• Things I can't change about my situation…
• Things I have learned from my situation…
• Ways I can think more positively about my situation…
• People who can help me improve my situation…
• Ways my family can grow due to this situation…
• My strengths that can help me improve my situation…

- Ways I can feel more certainty…
- Ways I can feel more variety, interest and excitement…
- Ways I can feel more respected, significant, important, unique and needed…
- Ways I can feel more connection and love…
- Ways I can feel like I am growing…
- Ways I can contribute to others…

Step 3. Ideas for action
- Write down all ideas you now have for actions you could take to change your situation.
- Make an action plan. Be specific, measurable, achievable, and realistic and timetable your actions.
- Then TAKE ACTION and review progress.

Vicky's situation

Vicky first came to see me, when her mother moved into her home, having just been told her cancer was in the terminal stages. Her mother had been sick for two years already, and Vicky was had already begun grieving. I helped Vicky adapt to her new role as caregiver for her mother, to the grief she was feeling and changes in her relationship with her husband, Steve and her two teenage sons. Much of this work focused on stress management techniques and organizational skills, to help with her new role.

Vicky returned to see me six weeks after her mother's death; for coaching on how what to do next. Her mother's illness had made her realize that she wanted to make more of her life, and she felt more resilient, more determined than ever. I helped Vicky come up with a plan to achieve three top goals: Save enough money to fund her sons through college, plan for early retirement and get down to her ideal weight. Vicky returned to work and with the help of a recommended financial planner, increased saving for her retirement, and college, for her boys. She and Steve rediscovered their love of hiking and made plans for several vacations, from their wish list.

Most people experience many adverse events and stressful situations, throughout their life. The outcome of these events is rarely set in stone. When you take personal responsibility for your life, accept that you deserve more happiness, health and success in your life, and take positive action; you can create a compelling future for you and your family.

Chapter 12 Summary

Your physical environment and situation have a significant impact on your wellbeing. Addressing problems with your situation or physical environment, can therefore, increase wellbeing for you and your family.

Physical environment includes your planet, country, locality and your home.

Many life events lead to a change in personal situation such as death and illness in the family, change in family dynamic, work and financial status.

It is possible to overcome most negative events or situations, and to become more resilient. This begins by accepting the situation, taking responsibility for your role in it and striving to make your life better. You deserve a truly great life, but ultimately your destiny is in your own hands.

Chapter 13

‿ YOUR FABULOUS ‿ FUTURE!

Congratulations you have made it through this book! I hope you have found *Beyond Soccer Mom* to be a powerful, thought provoking, challenging, energizing and inspirational experience. This chapter marks the end of this book, but not the end of your journey. In fact, it marks the beginning of an exciting, unpredictable and sometimes stormy journey that is the rest of your life. It is my sincere hope, that this book has guided you to some moments of clarity and self discovery, to make some important decisions and to take decisive action. I truly believe that all moms, especially those who have had the drive and determination to read this book, deserve to live remarkable lives.

Throughout the course of this book, I have given you advice, information and written exercises that have showed you how to increase wellbeing, in all areas of your life. Have you been doing the exercises throughout the book? If you have, fantastic, keep up the good work! If you haven't, I ask you "what's stopping you?" You have nothing to lose by doing these exercises and you'll be surprised by what you will gain. Go on, give them a try! Your success in achieving the life you deserve hinges on your positive, continued action.

If you have followed some or all of the principles and practiced some of the exercises in this book, it will have been a lot of hard work, but I am sure it will have been worth it. Take the time to acknowledge and congratulate yourself, on all you have done. We have covered a lot of ground, areas of your life and concepts. You now have a better understanding of who you are, at your core and know to trust your authentic self, to guide you to make excellent decisions. You have a clear vision of the changes you want to make in your life and a strategic plan on how to get there. Lastly, you should have learned to regulate your body and mind, so that it no longer sabotages your efforts; but instead supports them.

It is also my hope that the new improved you will have better relationships and become an inspirational role model for your whole family. Now that you have accepted that you deserve to be happy, healthy and successful, you will be able to better meet the needs of the people you love. Through your positive attitude and loving actions, your family will in turn learn that they too deserve happiness, health and success. They will see that they can achieve this by taking personal responsibility and affirmative action, towards their goals.

I urge you to continue with the good work, and to dip back into this book, using it like a recipe book, when the need arises. The reality is that life is going to continue to have its' ups and downs; but if you use this book wisely it will continue to be your guide, through some of these.

One final story

In April 2012, I attended "Unleash the Power Within", a four day, 50 hour Tony Robbins seminar. Here I gained focus, perspective, energy, drive, a plan and slightly burned feet (yes, I did the fire-walk!) The final day covered diet and lifestyle. As a physician and health coach, I knew much of the advice but for years had failed to follow it. When I got in my car, to leave, I said to myself "if I don't make this change now, I never will. SO I AM GOING TO COMMIT TO CHANGE NOW!" In the four months, that followed I changed to a plant based diet, rich in nutrition; I drank green smoothies for breakfast, rebounded, exercised and meditated daily. I watched the weight drop off. I felt great; people were telling me I looked amazing and I had more energy than when I was 20. Then I went back to visit family in England for three weeks. I allowed myself to stop exercising and start eating all my favorite British foods. On my return to the US, Super-storm Sandy hit. We had 10 days of limited power from a small generator, were forced to empty and eat the contents of our freezer, my boys were off school, and we had an evacuated family staying. All very stressful; not conducive to sensible eating. At the end of this, I had piled on 10lbs and was struggling to exercise. Then I had a health scare: One of those, where for a few awful days I thought I was going to die. That was all I needed to regain the drive and determination to get healthy. So I headed my own advice, from this book, did many of the exercises, regained focus, and got back to healthy habits. I realized that what had been missing, for me, was accountability. So I set up a community on Facebook called "Positive Steps to Health", through which I reinforce what I know, by sharing it with others and I gain support, inspiration and accountability from the group..

The moral of this story is that changing your life, is not simple and easy. Life often throws you a curve ball. I let some of the things that happened to me become excuses to return to old, bad habits. I used other events to gain strength and focus. This experience prompted me to set up a Facebook community to support you, in your ongoing journey, visit www.beyondsoccermom.com/community, for details on how to join.

The *Beyond Soccer Mom* experience does not end here; at www.beyondsoccermom.com you will continue to get support and advice, on all of the concepts in this book and much more. I invite you to explore the wealth of information, useful links and blog. If you want more help, need support and accountability or structure: You may like to take part in an online learning program, live event or work directly with me in a personal mentoring program. I look forward to being able to serve you, to empower you to create the awesome future, you and your family deserve.

Before we end, I have one last exercise for you. This is a mantra that will remind you of what you have learned in this book. Repeat it right now, and whenever you are feeling in need of a little personal power!

Exercise 13.1 Fabulous Me Mantra
Stand with your hand on your heart and say out loud:

"From this day forward I, (say your name) will live a life that is true to my authentic self. I deserve to live a wonderful life full of happiness, health, success and abundance. I take responsibility for my life. I am in control of my life. I will lead my family towards a fabulous future."

I offer you my sincere thanks for spending the time to read this book and travel the *Beyond Soccer Mom* journey, with me. I am honored that you have taken the time to read my book and follow my advice. I hope the experience has been a positive and empowering one and that it makes a difference in your life. Go out there and live an awesome future! Bye for now.

Leonaura

ABOUT THE AUTHOR

Dr Leonaura Rhodes is a Health and Happiness Coach, physician, neuroscience expert, speaker, author and busy mother.

As a coach Leonaura specializes in Health and Happiness Coaching and Strategic Neurocoaching. Her programs combine powerful coaching techniques, including Strategic Intervention, with neuroscience and medical expertise. She helps individuals and families overcome stress, illness and underachievement, by increasing health, happiness and success.

Leonaura brings to the table two decades of experience: as a physician in the UK, working with adults and children, in hospital medicine, general practice, public health medicine and developmental pediatrics and as a neuroscience expert; life coach and strategic interventionist. Leonaura also works as a freelance medical writer, combining her love of medicine and passion for writing.

Originally from England, Leonaura lives in Connecticut with her husband and two sons. She loves dancing, live concerts, kayaking and having adventures with her family!

REFERENCES

Books and Journals

Amen, Daniel G. *Change Your Brain, Change Your Body: Use Your Brain to Get and Keep the Body You Have Always Wanted: Boost Your Brain to Improve Your Weight, Skin, Heart, Energy, and Focus.* New York: Harmony Books, 2010.

Bstan-'dzin-rgya-mtsho, and Howard C. Cutler. *The Art of Happiness: A Handbook for Living.* New York: Riverhead Books, 1998.

Cacioppo, John T, and William Patrick. *Loneliness: Human Nature and the Need for Social Connection.* New York: W.W. Norton & Co, 2008.

Clair Et Al. "Association of Smoking Cessation and Weight Change with Cardiovascular Disease among Adults with and without Diabetes." *JAMA* (2013)

Cohen, Carol F, and Vivian S. Rabin. *Back on the Career Track: A Guide for Stay-at-Home Moms Who Want to Return to Work.* New York: Business Plus, 2007.

Duhigg, Charles. *The Power of Habit: Why We Do What We Do in Life and Business.* New York: Random House, 2012.

Frech, A. "The Relationships between Mothers' Work Pathways and Physical and Mental Health." *J Health Soc Behav.* 2012;53(4):396-412

Gottman, John M, and Nan Silver. *The Seven Principles for Making Marriage Work.* New York: Crown Publishers, 1999.

Hardy, Darren. *The Compound Effect: Multiplying Your Success, One Simple Step at a Time.* New York, NY: Vanguard Press, 2010.

Hinshaw, Stephen P. *Origins of the Human Mind.* Chantilly, Va: Teaching Co, 2010.

Ironside, Virginia. *The Huge Bag of Worries.* Macdonald Young Books, 1998.

Kiyosaki, Kim. *It's Rising Time!: A Call for Women : What It Really Takes for the Reward of Financial Freedom.* Scottsdale, AZ: Plata Pub, 2011.

Kiyosaki, Robert T. *Rich Dad's Increase Your Financial Iq: Get Smarter with Your Money.* New York: Business Plus, 2008.

Kiyosaki, Robert T. *Unfair Advantage: The Power of Financial Education : What Schools Will Never Teach You About Money.* Scottsdale, AZ: Plata Pub, 2011.

Miklush L, Connelly CD. Maternal Depression and Infant Development: Theory and Current Evidence. Am J Matern Child Nurs. 2013 Aug 28.

Orman, Suze. *Women & Money: Owning the Power to Control Your Destiny.* New York: Spiegel & Grau, 2007.

Quigley, Mary W., and Loretta Kaufman. *Going Back to Work: A Survival Guide for Comeback Moms.* New York: St. Martin's Griffin, 2004.

Rath, Tom. *Strengths Finder 2.0.* New York: Gallup Press, 2007.

Siegel, Daniel J. *Mindsight: The New Science of Personal Transformation.* New York: BantamBooks, 2011.

The Advantages of Being a Working MotherSunstone Online, http://www.sunstoneonline.com/the-advantages-of-being-a-working-mother (accessed January 2, 2014).

Thouless, Robert Henry. *Teach Yourself Straight and Crooked Thinking.* London: Teach Yourself, 2010.

Tracy, Brian. *Eat That Frog!: 21 Great Ways to Stop Procrastinating and Get More Done in Less Time.* San Francisco, CA: Berrett-Koehler Publishers, 2001.

Ware, Bronnie. *The Top Five Regrets of the Dying: A Life Transformed by the Dearly Departing.* Carlsbad, CA: Hay House, 2012. Print.

Weih, M., J. Wiltfang, and J. Kornhuber. "Non-pharmacologic Prevention of Alzheimer's Disease: Nutritional and Life-style Risk Factors." *Journal of Neural Transmission* 114.9 (2007): 1187-197.

Wladis Hoffman, Lois. "The Effects of the Mother's Employment on the Family and the Child." *The Effects of the Mother's Employment on the Family and the Child.* Parenthood In America, 15 Oct. 1998.

Online sources

www.blogs.hbr.org/2012/12/new-research-the-skills-that-m/

www.experiencelife.com/article/how-healthy-people-shop/

www.forbes.com/sites/ericwagner/2012/06/05/7-traits-of-incredibly-successful-entrepreneurs/>

www.iom.edu/Reports/2004/Dietary-Reference-Intakes-Water-Potassium-Sodium-Chloride-and-Sulfate.aspx

www.mayoclinic.com/health/empty-nest-syndrome/MY01976

www.nhlbi.nih.gov/health/health-topics/topics/obe/causes.html

www.prweb.com/releases/2011/5/prweb8393658.htm

www.uakron.edu/im/online-newsroom/news_details.dot?newsId=b4817895-3ebf-4fcb-bf5c-ad482e292d25&crumbTitle=Work%20has%20more%20benefits%20than%20just%20a%20paycheck%20for%20moms

CPSIA information can be obtained at www.ICGtesting.com
Printed in the USA
BVOW04s1552031114

373089BV00001B/1/P